THE PRIEST AS BELOVED SON

EDITED BY DEACON JAMES KEATING, PH.D.

THE INSTITUTE FOR PRIESTLY FORMATION
IPF PUBLICATIONS

CONTRIBUTORS

Suzanne Baars, Ph.D. is a licensed professional counselor and marriage and family therapist who operates In His Image Christian Counseling Center in Irving, Texas.

Fr. Earl K. Fernandes, Ph.D. is Dean of Mount St. Mary's Seminary in Cincinnati, Ohio.

Fr. David Vincent Meconi, S.J. is Assistant Professor of Theological Studies at St. Louis University in St. Louis, Missouri.

Fr. Walter R. Oxley, S.T.D., S.T.L. is an Associate Professor, Vice Rector for Formation, Dean of Community Life, and Director of Human Formation for the School of Theology at the Pontifical College Josephinum in Columbus, Ohio.

Margaret M. Turek, S.T.D. is the leader of Faith Formation and Catechesis for the Diocese of Oakland, Calfornia.

Peter S. Williamson, S.T.D. holds the Adam Cardinal Maida Chair in Sacred Scripture at Sacred Heart Major Seminary in Detroit, Michigan.

.

.

THE INSTITUTE FOR PRIESTLY FORMATION
IPF Publications
2500 California Plaza
Omaha, Nebraska 68178
www.IPFPublications.com

Printed in the United States of America
ISBN-13: 978-0-9887613-4-6

Cover design by Timothy D. Boatright
Marketing Associates, USA
Tampa, Florida

THE INSTITUTE FOR PRIESTLY FORMATION
MISSION STATEMENT

The Institute for Priestly Formation was founded to assist bishops in the spiritual formation of diocesan seminarians and priests in the Roman Catholic Church. The Institute responds to the need to foster spiritual formation as the integrating and governing principle of all aspects for priestly formation. Inspired by the biblical-evangelical spirituality of Ignatius Loyola, this spiritual formation has as its goal the cultivation of a deep interior communion with Christ; from such communion, the priest shares in Christ's own pastoral charity. In carrying out its mission, the Institute directly serves diocesan seminarians and priests as well as those who are responsible for diocesan priestly formation.

THE INSTITUTE FOR PRIESTLY FORMATION
Creighton University
2500 California Plaza
Omaha, Nebraska 68178
www.priestlyformation.org
ipf@creighton.edu

TABLE OF CONTENTS

FOREWORD

I recently asked a seminarian who had just come from a retreat if his experience had been fruitful. He relayed without hesitation and with glowing excitement that, "The truth that I am the beloved son of the Father has changed everything." The experience of receiving the Father's love in an ever new, profound, and intimate way does indeed "change everything" and is a foundational grace which is crucial for each seminarian to assimilate as he moves toward spiritual fatherhood in his priestly call. In my thirteen years of forming men for the priesthood, it has become abundantly clear that helping seminarians become "beloved sons" needs to have a central place in spiritual development and seminary formation.

It is no mystery that there are many challenges to priestly formation today and many demands to ensure that seminarians, who come from a great variety of family, spiritual, and cultural backgrounds, are adequately prepared for ministry. Each seminary would be wise to ensure that there is an intentional effort at incorporating into the spiritual formation program a path where each man can mature with an experience of beloved sonship as its foundation. The exceptional essays which follow can be of great assistance in achieving that end because they expound upon the extraordinary spiritual richness contained in the identity and truth of beloved sonship. These writings could be used as a continuing formation tool for faculty and staff with the goal of ensuring that each seminarian be given the proper guidance and formation in becoming a beloved son of our Heavenly Father.

Msgr. Robert J. Panke, STL
Rector
Saint John Paul II Seminary, Washington, D.C.

Scriptural Foundations for the Priest as Beloved Son

Peter S. Williamson

Introduction

Of the various "identities" that define a priest, that of "beloved son" of God is the most fundamental. It is an identity that priests share with the rest of the Christian faithful.

Personally discovering one's identity as a son or daughter of God is a grace that makes an immense difference for any Christian. It did for me. I was a typical nineteen-year-old with the insecurities and self-image problems common to that time of life. I was overly aware of my shortcomings, worried what people thought of me, and searching to discover who I really was. I belonged to an ecumenical prayer group; and one evening, our guest speaker was an Episcopalian priest. Using texts from Paul, he taught that we are sons of God because God has poured the Spirit of His Son into us, enabling us to address God as "Abba, Father!" (Gal 4:6). He preached the words spoken to Jesus at His Baptism, "You are my beloved Son; with you I am well pleased" (Lk 3:22). At the beginning and at the end of the priest's message, he prayed that the Holy Spirit would communicate this truth to our hearts. Then, he taught us a chorus that repeats the words, "I am a son of God; I am a son of God; I am a son of God; His Spirit lives in me." I could not get that song out of my mind, not only because of a catchy melody, but because that truth had lodged itself deeply in my heart. I realized that I have a relationship with God that no one can take away and that I have an extraordinary future when my identity as a son of God will be fully revealed (Rom 8:19; 1 Jn 3:2). I realized that our heavenly Father loves me, that His pleasure rests on me, that He is *for* me. Compared to that knowledge, what others might think or say about me does not matter. My self-image problems did not disappear all at once, but the discovery that I am a son of God changed me.[1]

Jesus' relationship with the Father was announced at His Baptism; Luke offers the most succinct account:

> After all the people had been baptized and Jesus also had been baptized and was praying, heaven was opened and the holy Spirit descended upon him in bodily form like a dove. And a voice came from heaven, "You are my beloved Son; with you I am well pleased." (Lk 3:21-22)

Luke, alone, reports that Jesus received this revelation when He was praying. Although Jesus understood His divine sonship from childhood (as His words to Mary at the finding in the temple indicate), Jesus *grew* in wisdom, like the rest of us who share His human nature (Lk 2:52). Luke and Mark report the voice from heaven as directly addressing Jesus: "*You* are my beloved Son…"(emphasis author's). A father's love and approval is very precious; I remember the occasions on which my father expressed his love and approval of me.

What joy and encouragement the Father's words must have brought to Jesus.

It is worth observing that the expression of God's pleasure in Jesus on this occasion was not primarily a response to Jesus' achievement or performance to date, but rather a manifestation of the Father's favor toward His son. The words recall Isaiah 42:1: "Here is my servant whom I uphold, my chosen one with whom I am pleased. Upon him I have put my spirit; he shall bring forth justice to the nations."

The significance of these words of God to Jesus increases when we learn more about the relationship of fathers and sons in first-century Palestine. The eldest son was raised to assume his father's responsibility for the family farm or business and his position in the community. Typically, fathers apprenticed their sons to do what they did. A son lived with or near his father and worked with him on a daily basis. Jesus alludes to this relationship in John 5:19-23 where He speaks of the Father showing the Son what He does, and the Son doing only what He sees the Father doing. As the heir, the firstborn adult son was regarded in the community as having honor like that of his father, which is why Jesus' claim to be God's Son was taken as making himself equal to God (Jn 5:18). Often, though not always, the relationship between father and son was the closest family relationship, closer in many ways than the relationship between husband and wife.[2]

Of course, Jesus is God's Son in an altogether unique way. Scripture speaks in a variety of ways about human beings as sons and daughters of God. In this essay, I will briefly survey what the Old Testament says before presenting the New Testament teaching on the subject in the writings of Paul and

John. I will conclude with a word about Christian experience
and how priests and seminarians can grow in their identity as
beloved sons of the Father.

Son of God in the Old Testament

A few verses after the Baptism of Jesus, another son of
God is mentioned. At the end of Jesus' genealogy, we read
the names of Jesus' earliest ancestors: "Enos, the son of Seth,
the son of Adam, the son of God" (Lk 3: 38). Luke, thus,
teaches that Adam, and the human race descended from him,
is God's son. In fact, the Old Testament in various places
refers to Adam, Israel, and the kings of Israel as God's son.

Adam

Although Genesis does not explicitly call Adam and the
human race "the son of God," Genesis depicts Adam's relationship with God as a filial relationship. God provides Adam
with land, an occupation, and a wife and places Adam in
authority over all His possessions as His representative—just
what a good father in the ancient Near East would do for
his son. Furthermore, Genesis describes human beings, both
male and female, as being created "in the image of God"
(1:27). A few chapters later, Genesis uses this language to
refer to Adam's son Seth: "Adam was one hundred and thirty
years old when he begot a son in his likeness, after his image;
and he named him Seth" (Gn 5:3).

Although, in the beginning, God created the human race
to be in a family relationship with Him, for us to be His sons
and daughters, and corporately to be His son, it is not an
accident that the Old Testament does not develop this idea
very much. The fall of man and the subsequent wickedness

of the human race imposed a seemingly insuperable obstacle to human capacity for familial intimacy with God.

Israel

A handful of other Old Testament texts refer to Israel, the descendants of Abraham, as God's son. Before the Exodus, God instructs Moses to tell Pharaoh: "Thus says the LORD: Israel is my son, my firstborn. I said to you: Let my son go, that he may serve me" (Ex 4:22-23). God recalls this event through the prophet Hosea: "When Israel was a child I loved him, out of Egypt I called my son" (Hos 11:1). Deuteronomy 32:5-6 indicates God is Israel's Father because He created Israel, although Israel's perverse conduct disqualifies Israel from being His son. After Israel and Judah go into exile for their sins, the Lord remembers His son and through Jeremiah, promises mercy to a chastened Israel whom He describes as pleasing and obedient: "Is Ephraim not my favored son, the child in whom I delight? Even though I threaten him, I must still remember him! My heart stirs for him, I must show him compassion!—oracle of the Lord" (Jer 31:20—LXX 38:20).

The Son of David

If Israel is God's "firstborn" among the nations God fathered, it is logical that the king of Israel, God's delegated authority, should also be recognized as God's son. God, therefore, promises to adopt David's royal descendants.

When your days have been completed and you rest with your ancestors, I will raise up your offspring after you, sprung from your loins, and I will establish his kingdom. He it is who shall build a house for my name, and I will establish his royal throne forever. I will be a father to him, and he shall be a son to me. (2 Sm 7:12-14)

The short-term fulfillment of this prophecy was that Solomon and his successors in the Davidic line were regarded as adopted sons of God. A royal psalm celebrates this unique relationship in the famous words, "I will proclaim the decree of the Lord, 'You are my son; today I have begotten you. Ask it of me, and I will give you the nations as your inheritance, and, as your possession, the ends of the earth . . .'" (Ps 2:7-8). The special relationship as God's adopted sons that David and his descendants enjoyed qualified them to perform priestly functions (2 Sam 6:14; 8:18; 1 Kings 8) and to be described in Psalm 110:4 as belonging to a special priestly order, the order of Melchizedek.

The "Beloved Son" in the Old Testament: Isaac

Before leaving the Old Testament, it is important to note a text that anticipates the expression "beloved son," although it refers not to a son of God but a son of Abraham. The Septuagint version of Genesis 22 refers to Isaac as Abraham's beloved son three times, using the same Greek words pronounced by the voice from heaven at Jesus' Baptism. God tells Abraham, "Take your son Isaac, your only one, whom you love" (Gn 22:2), and offer him as a sacrifice. Then later, "I know that you fear God, since you did not withhold from me your son" (Gn 22:12), which leads God to swear an oath to bless him with many descendants and to give him victory over his enemies (Gn 22: 16-18). Jesus is God's Isaac, the unique son whom He loves. Like Isaac, Jesus trusts His Father, surrenders His life, and receives it back.

Adam, Israel, the sons of David, and Isaac are all types of the beloved Son of the Father who was to be revealed in the fullness of time. A few years ago, someone taught me this helpful principle of Christian biblical interpretation: Christ recapitulates the history of Israel; the Christian is called to recapitulate the life of Christ. Jesus recapitulates Israel's history in a way that perfects and completes it. He is the new Adam who obeys, the new Israel who keeps the Torah, the new David who will rule all nations forever, and the new Isaac, the beloved Son of the Father, who willingly lays down His life. In the New Testament, Paul teaches that baptized believers recapitulate the life of Christ as God's Son, not merely by imitation but by participation in His divine sonship.

New Testament: Sons in the Son, Galatians 4:3-7

The Gentile Christians of Galatia had been persuaded by some Jews of the circumcision party that faith in Christ was not enough to fully belong to God's covenant people. They needed to become Jews by accepting circumcision and observing the law of Moses. Paul responds by saying that incorporation into Christ through faith and Baptism not only makes them Abraham's offspring (since Christ is Abraham's descendant), it also makes them sons of God (Gal 3:26-29). Then, he explains how both Jews and Gentiles, previously subject to the elementary powers of the world, have attained a new standing because God intervened, sending His Son and sending the Holy Spirit:

> But when the fullness of time had come, God sent his Son, born of a woman, born under the law, to ransom those under the law, so that we might receive adoption. As proof that you are children, God sent the spirit of his

Son into our hearts, crying out, "Abba! Father!" So you are no longer a slave but a son, and if a child then also an heir, through God. (Gal 4:4-7)

Adoption was not practiced among Jews but was somewhat widely practiced in the Greco-Roman world. According to Roman law, an adopted son or daughter had all the legal rights of a biological child. Paul, however, does not stop at speaking of a mere legal adoption that would not interiorly change the person who is adopted. Instead, he speaks of a decisive divine intervention that communicates a new life, participation in the filial life of the Risen Christ: "As proof that you are children, God sent the spirit of his Son into our hearts, crying out, 'Abba! Father!'" (Gal 4:6) It is Jesus' own Spirit that we receive.

Paul supports his claim from Christian experience by saying that the Spirit of the Son of God that his readers have received cries, "Abba! Father!" *Abba* is an Aramaic word used by sons and daughters in a family setting to address their father. It was not common for Jews to address their all-powerful and all-holy God in prayer with this familiar language. *Abba* is found only three times in the New Testament: here, in a parallel text about sonship (Rom 8:15), and on the lips of Jesus during His agony in the garden in Mark 14:36. Paul's argument presupposes that his Christian readers both in Galatia and in Rome, a Church he had not yet visited, were accustomed to using this Aramaic loanword to address God as Father. The most plausible explanation is that Jesus used this word in prayer and taught His disciples, who spread the practice in the apostolic Church, to do the same.[3]

It is not obvious in English, but in the original Greek of Galations 4:7—"So you are no longer a slave but a child, and if a child then also an heir, through God"—Paul switches from addressing his readers in the second person plural to the second person singular, making clear that this truth applies to every individual Christian. In effect, he is proclaiming to every Christian, "*You* are no longer a slave.... to sin, to the law, to people's opinions, to your weaknesses, to the devil, to the world. Instead, *you* are a free man, a free woman, a son or daughter of God." Paul goes further. "*You* are an heir. Your sonship entails a right to the inheritance." According to other passages in Paul (Eph 1:14; 2 Cor 1:22; 5:5), the gift of the Spirit that Christians receive now is a first installment on their inheritance, a guarantee and a foretaste that assures them of the good things that God has for them in the age to come.

Christian Experience and Future Transformation, Romans 8:14-23, 29

In Romans, Paul explains the consequences of justification and the role of the Holy Spirit.

> For those who are led by the Spirit of God are children of God. For you did not receive a spirit of slavery to fall back into fear, but you received a spirit of adoption, through which we cry, "Abba, Father!" The Spirit itself bears witness with our spirit that we are children of God . . . (Rom 8:14-16)

Paul begins with Christian experience of the Spirit. Paul presupposes that his readers know what it means to be led by the Spirit, just as Matthew and Luke report that the Spirit led Jesus into the desert after His Baptism. Paul presupposes that his readers have come to experience God as Father, that the Holy Spirit bears an interior witness that they are children of God.[4] When they pray the Our Father, or otherwise pray to God, they experience God as their Father.

It is significant that in this text, Paul speaks of "the Spirit of God," while in his letter to the Galations, he speaks of "the spirit of his Son" (4:6). In Romans 8:9, Paul explicitly identifies the Spirit of God—known from the Old Testament—with the Spirit of Christ.[5] Paul, thus, unveils something profound about the inner life of the Trinity, that the Father and the Son possess one Spirit. A person's spirit is his inmost self (see 1 Cor 2:10-16); the Father and the Son are united by sharing one Spirit. The implication for the Christian's relationship to God is also profound. By being adopted and given the Spirit of the Son, which is also the Spirit of God the Father, we are intimately united to the Father and the Son because at the center of our being dwells their same Spirit.

Next, Paul states an important condition of receiving our filial inheritance: "if only we suffer with him so that we may also be glorified with him" (Rom 8:17). Sons in the Son through faith and Baptism and called to recapitulate the life of Christ, Christians share in His sufferings. The good news is that our sufferings in this life "are as nothing compared with the glory to be revealed for us" (Rom 8:18).

Then, Paul indicates the extraordinary dignity that belongs to the children of God:

> For creation awaits with eager expectation the revelation of the children of God; for creation was made subject to futility, not of its own accord but because of the one

who subjected it, in hope that creation itself would be set free from slavery to corruption and share in the glorious freedom of the children of God. (Rom 8:19-21)

The well-being of creation, of the earth, of the animal world, of the stars, is intimately tied to that of the human race (Gen 3:17-19). When human beings became guilty of moral evil, physical evil in the universe (tsunamis, disease, hurricanes, etcetera) was one of the results. When Christ returns and our glory as sons of God is revealed, creation itself will be liberated. Paul's words imply that our identity as sons of God is now hidden, something he states explicitly in Col 3:3-4: "For you have died, and your life is hidden with Christ in God. When Christ your life appears, then you too will appear with him in glory." Far from being mere legal adoptees, as sons and daughters, we participate in God's divine life. The second coming of Christ will result in the manifestation of our true identity.

Paul contrasts our present struggle with this future glory which he also describes as "adoption as sons":

We know that all creation is groaning in labor pains even until now; and not only that, but we ourselves, who have the firstfruits of the Spirit, we also groan within ourselves as we wait for adoption, the redemption of our bodies. (Rom 8:22-23)

Paul, thus, distinguishes two phases of our adopted sonship, one that is already ours ("the firstfruits"), and another that we await ("the redemption of our bodies"). While our inmost selves, our spirits, have been redeemed by Christ and transformed by the gift of the Spirit, our weak bodies and fallen human nature inherited from Adam will receive a total makeover when Christ returns. Paul describes the goal of this process in Romans 8:29: "For those he foreknew he also predestined to be conformed to the image of his Son, so that he might be the firstborn among many brothers."[6]

So our sonship is very real in the deepest part of our being, yet we live in bodies that are not yet fully redeemed. Paul describes this struggle within us between the spirit and the flesh in Galations 5:16-25.

The Confirming Testimony of the Johannine Literature

In a very different manner of speaking, John, the other great theologian of the New Testament, teaches the same wonderful truths about our identity and glorious future as God's sons and daughters. Rather than employ the metaphor of adoption, John speaks of rebirth: "But to those who did accept him he gave power to become children of God, to those who believe in his name, who were born not by natural generation nor by human choice nor by a man's decision but of God" (John 1:12-13). John also speaks of rebirth in chapter 3, verses 5-7: "Amen, amen, I say to you, no one can enter the kingdom of God without being born of water and spirit. Do not be amazed that I told you, 'You must be born from above.'"

Like Paul, John speaks of our sonship as a hidden reality—the world cannot see our true identity: "See what love the Father has bestowed on us that we may be called the children of God. Yet so we are. The reason the world does not know us is that it did not know him" (1 John 3:1).

John also speaks of a future transformation: "Beloved, we are God's children now; what we shall be has not yet been revealed. We do know that when it is revealed we shall be like him, for we shall see him as he is" (1 Jn 3:2).

John teaches, as Paul does, that becoming sons of God changes our conduct. While Paul speaks of the Spirit as the source of this change, John emphasizes the new nature that results from a new birth: "No one who is begotten by God commits sin, because God's seed remains in him; he cannot sin because he is begotten by God" (1 Jn 3:9).[7] He uses a startling metaphor to describe the ontological difference that characterizes the Christian: "God's seed," literally, his *sperma*, "remains in him."

Experience of the Spirit

It is clear from the New Testament that for the apostolic Church, the gift of the Holy Spirit that confirms the Christian's identity as a son or daughter of God was not an abstract doctrine but *a fact of experience* (see especially Acts 8:14-18; 10:44-46; 19:6).[8] Christian initiation was a radically life-transforming event with perceptible outward effects, including an experiential awareness of the Father's love and the lordship of Christ (Rom 5:5; 8:15-16; 1 Cor 12:3).[9] The fact is that many Catholics, including many priests and seminarians, have not experienced the Holy Spirit in the way that Paul's and John's readers considered normal (see Gal 3:2-4).

The universality of that experience in the early Church was due to a variety of factors. Most Church members were adult converts who personally responded to the preaching of the Gospel and were initiated into Spirit-filled communities whose identity and way of life differed sharply from the surrounding society. It is not surprising that today, people baptized as infants who grow up in a secular culture do not automatically arrive at the same vital experience of the Holy Spirit. The dispositions necessary for Baptism and Confirmation to bear fruit include a lively understanding of the Gospel and the gifts God intends for His people, personal faith in Jesus, repentance, and the desire to do God's will. If someone who received the sacraments as an infant grows up in a vibrant community of faith, the effects of the sacraments unfold naturally as these dispositions develop. However, to the degree that Christians baptized as infants and confirmed as adolescents do not acquire these dispositions, the grace of those sacraments often remains dormant and unfruitful.[10] In the part of his *Summa Theologica* devoted to Baptism (III, Q. 66-71), Thomas Aquinas indicates the importance of adequate preparation and the proper dispositions for the efficacy of Baptism, including repentance and faith, devotion, sincerity, instruction, exorcism, and the presence of responsible godparents.[11] In the aggressively secular environment the Church faces around the world today, pastoral care cannot be content with merely administering valid sacraments, but must aim to lead Catholics to the fruit proper to each sacrament.

Increasingly, thanks be to God, Catholics are rediscovering the importance of inviting everyone to a personal relationship with Jesus Christ and to a vital relationship with the Holy Spirit. Excellent means, such as Ignatian retreats, Cursillo, the Life in the Spirit Seminar, the Philip course (http://www.metanoiaproject.co.uk/philip/philip.htm), and the Alpha Course have been found effective in initiating Catholics into the kind of experiential relationship with God that enables them to perceive the action of the Holy Spirit in their lives.[12] After this fruit of Baptism and Confirmation has been personally experienced, then the biblical teaching about identity as sons and daughters of God becomes intelligible, since it explains something about Christian experience.

The Priest as Beloved Son

Paul's Letter to the Hebrews argues that it is fitting that Christ should be our high priest because of His intimate solidarity both with human beings and with God. Priestly mediation requires that a priest have a vital relationship both with God and with the people he is serving. Christ is united to us because He has taken on our nature and been tempted as we are tempted (Heb 2:10-18). He is united to God by being God's Son (Heb 1:5; 2:5-6; 3:5-6; 7:26-28). Christians share in Christ's priesthood, united to other people by their common humanity and, to God, by being sons in the Son.

An ordained priest, like every Christian, is a son of the Father in Christ, the Beloved Son, graced with the Holy Spirit that gives him the heart of the Father and mind of Christ. His sonship is essential for his priestly ministry since, united with Christ our High priest, an ordained priest serves as a mediator between God and mankind. He is also called to help all the people of God discover and live out their identity as beloved sons and daughters.

What, therefore, must distinguish priests in living as beloved sons of God is a deep experiential understanding of their identity as God's sons that will enable them to lead the faithful into the same knowledge and experience. What must also characterize priests is a deep decision to live like Jesus as God's beloved sons, conformed as much as possible to Christ's obedient love for the Father and His unlimited love for His brother and sisters. That filial obedience and love is what characterized Paul, John, and the apostles.

I would like to conclude with three practical suggestions for how seminarians and priests can grow in their identity as beloved sons of the Father.

First, they can seek to grow in their relationship with the Holy Spirit, since one of the important reasons we received the Spirit was to manifest our true identity and relationship with God and Christ. Paul exhorts the Ephesians to be filled with the Holy Spirit and describes Spirit-filled worship and character (Eph 5:18-21; Gal 5:22-23). Priests and seminarians can ask the Father to give them more of His Holy Spirit, a prayer that Jesus specially commends and promises will be granted (Lk 11:9-13). St. John Paul II prayed daily for the grace of the Holy Spirit, using a prayer his father had taught him when he was a boy. Developing one's relationship with the Spirit entails learning to recognize and discern the leadings and inspirations of the Spirit in daily life, a habit about which Ignatius Loyola and other spiritual writers of the past and present teach us. Finally, they can learn to let the Spirit inspire their prayer in the Liturgy and privately, whether through praying Scripture, the gift of tears, the charism of tongues, or "inexpressible groanings" (Rom 8:26).

Second, priests and seminarians can read, study, meditate on, and memorize Sacred Scripture. In several places, Paul teaches that we are transformed by the renewing of our minds (Rom 12:2; Eph 4:23; Col 3:10). Reading and reflecting on Scripture is the very best way for our minds to be renewed so that we can think with the mind of Christ. This conviction was recently confirmed when a seminarian approached me after a Pauline Literature class with his face glowing. He expressed fervent agreement with what I had just taught from Romans about our being sons of God, and he shared how his whole outlook had changed the previous summer at The Institute for Priestly Formation when his spiritual director gave him some texts on which to meditate. At my request, he later e-mailed me the texts and wrote:

> The main thing that I have received from these texts is the reality that I am a beloved Son of the Father by the grace of God through Baptism, and that the life I live is a sharing in the life of Christ. I learned about sonship, the future redemption of creation, the Fatherhood of God, the divine indwelling, the Beatitudes, and the motherhood of Mary. Please note that the graces I received came from meditating on these texts one at a time, praying with each one for an hour and returning to some of them as directed by my spiritual director.
>
> My identity as a beloved son and as a Christian was strengthened because of the Word, which is a soothing ointment. I am better disposed now to receive God's grace and the gifts of the Holy Spirit. My house is better ordered.[13]

After a priest or seminarian has grasped interiorly the wonderful truth of his identity as a beloved son in the Son, he will want to live in filial intimacy through an obedience to the Father, like that of Jesus. To deepen this grace, I recommend reading the Gospel of John and meditating on the words Jesus speaks about His relationship to the Father. Likewise, I recommend reading Hebrews, reflecting on the passages that speak of Jesus' sonship, obedience, suffering, and priesthood.

Realizing one's identity as a son of God may have a marked beginning point, as it did for me; but growth in that awareness can deepen throughout our lives until Christ returns and changes us fully into His likeness. Even then, eternity may not be long enough to appreciate what it means that God has made us beloved sons and daughters.

NOTES

1. This paragraph is adapted from a reflection I wrote in Peter S. Williamson, *Ephesians*, Catholic Commentary on Sacred Scripture 3 (Grand Rapids, MI: Baker, 2009), 35-36.

2. For an illuminating discussion of fathers and sons in the first century and the implications as such for Christ as Son of God and High Priest, see Stephen B. Clark, *Redeemer: Understanding the Meaning of the Life, Death and Resurrection of Jesus Christ* (Ann Arbor: Servant, 1992), 165-168, available from Tabor House (http://www.sos-nar.com/tabor.htm).

3. In a similar way, a few Hebrew loanwords, such as *Amen, Alleluia*, and *Sabaoth*, made their way into Greek and Latin Liturgy.

4. Paul passes easily from speaking of being "sons of God" to the inclusive "children of God," indicating that his meaning has been inclusive all along. In 2 Cor 6:18, Paul quotes Hos 1:10, but changes "sons" to "sons and daughters of the living God."

5. "But you are not in the flesh; on the contrary, you are in the spirit, if only the Spirit of God dwells in you. Whoever does not have the Spirit of Christ does not belong to him" (Rom 8:9).

6. Paul tells how this will come about in 1 Cor 15:51-53: "Behold, I tell you a mystery. We shall not all fall asleep, but we will all be changed, in an instant, in the blink of an eye, at the last trumpet. For the trumpet will sound, the dead will be raised incorruptible, and we shall be changed. For that which is corruptible must clothe itself with incorruptibility, and that which is mortal must clothe itself with immortality."

7. In one version of the Bible, this quote is: "No one born of God makes a practice of sinning, for God's seed abides in him, and he cannot keep on sinning because he has been born of God" The use of present participles in the previous three verses of that version and of a present infinitive in this verse, indicates a continuous or habitual action (*New American Bible*, English Standard Version: "makes a practice of sinning"), rather than a single action (*New American Bible*, Revised Standard Version: "commits sin").

8. The fact that this is the case in both the New Testament and the patristic era is demonstrated by Kilian McDonnell and George T. Montague, *Christian Initiation and Baptism in the Spirit: Evidence from the First Eight Centuries*, 2nd ed. (Collegeville, Minn.: Liturgical Press, 1994).

9. Other perceptible effects of faith and Baptism in the New Testament included joy in their salvation (Acts 8:5-8; Rom 15:13; 1 Pet 1:8), overflowing praise (Acts 2:11, 46-47), an eagerness to know the Apostles' teaching (Acts 2:42), zeal to boldly proclaim Christ (Acts 4:31; 9:20; 1 Cor 9:16), and service to others through various charisms of the Spirit (1 Cor 12:7-13).

10.   See Raniero Cantalamessa, *Sober Intoxication of the Spirit* (Cincinnati: St. Anthony Messenger, 2005), 41-49.

11.   Ralph Martin has recently published two articles related to attaining the fruit of the Sacraments of Initiation: "The Post-Christendom Sacramental Crisis: the Wisdom of St. Thomas Aquinas" (*Nova et Vetera* 11:1 [2013], 57-75) and "New Pentecost? Catholic Theology and Baptism in the Spirit" (*Logos: A Journal of Catholic Thought and Culture* 4:13 [Summer 2011], 17-43). Both are available online at www.RenewalMinistries.net under "Free Resources."

12.   A number of seminaries in the United States and abroad have begun using these evangelization programs as part of their program of formation.

13.   Here are the texts the seminarian shared with me: on sonship, Rom 8:14-39 and Gal 4:4-7; on the divine indwelling, Gal 2:19-20; on rejoicing and peace, Phil 4:4-9; on the nature of concupiscence, Rom 7; on sharing in the life of Christ, Col 3:1-4; on pursuing Christ, Phil 3:7-14; on courage and confidence, 2 Tim 1:1-12.

ST. THOMAS AQUINAS AND AFFECTIVE MATURITY

SUZANNE BAARS

The subject of affective maturity holds a special relevance to the formation of seminarians, the life of the priest, and the priesthood itself. Moreover, the anthropology of St. Thomas Aquinas, specifically his conception of the integral role of the passions for the life of virtue, demonstrates the psychic integration necessary for the mature development of the human person, as well as for his personal happiness. This is particularly important for the priest, who will become a spiritual father to many persons.

The authentic anthropology of St. Thomas Aquinas was largely ignored for centuries, due to an unfortunate prejudice against the emotions as leading people toward sin. The doctrine developed by two Catholic psychiatrists, Dr. Anna Terruwe and Dr. Conrad Baars, is based on St. Thomas's treatise on human nature which explains the relation of the emotions to reason and will. Moreover, Terruwe made the important discovery of deprivation neurosis (or Emotional Deprivation Disorder) in which she postulated that a deprivation of love could generate a neurosis. Together, she and Baars showed that healing of this deprivation comes through the genuine affirmation of the person. This essay will illustrate why Pope Paul VI declared Dr. Terruwe's work to be "a gift to the Church."[1]

St. Thomas Aquinas's Understanding of the Passions and Virtue

St. Thomas Aquinas said, "A passion of the soul increases the goodness of an action."[2] Paul Glenn paraphrases, "A good act performed with feeling as well as with intention is all the better for thus coming more completely from the whole man."[3] The Catechism of the Catholic Church says, "The human person is ordered to beatitude by his deliberate acts: the passions or feelings he experiences can dispose him to it and contribute to it."[4] Taken together, one may conclude that to develop the capacity to experience and respond to feelings and emotions is crucial for the integration of the person, as the passions even participate in the development of the habits of virtue.

By way of illustration, St. Thomas judges the moral character of a person not solely by what he or she does or does not do, but by the fact that he finds pleasure or joy in the good (or evil) that he does. He states that virtue is not only in the will and reason, but also in the emotions.[5] Some exemplars of this concept would be St. John Paul II and Blessed Teresa of Calcutta: what one saw in their faces was their delight in the people they met. Their feelings were evident in their countenance and were an integral part of their gift of self. Others were delighted by and attracted to them, and their joy often moved others to love in return. To the contrary, the opposite of this would be someone who commits a heinous crime and *takes pleasure in* hurting someone else. Not only is

this an evil act in itself, but it evokes a corresponding sense
of repugnance and revulsion toward the evildoer. Our own
emotional reactions mirror what we sense about the person.

Thus, what St. Thomas refers to is not merely a judgment
of behavior, but takes into consideration the desire of the
person and his object as indicative of either a virtuous or
vicious nature. The Catechism further quotes St. Thomas's
thought on this matter: "Moral perfection consists in man's
being moved to the good not by his will alone, but also by
his sensitive appetite, as in the words of the psalm: 'My heart
and flesh sing for joy to the living God:' (Psalm 84:2) whereby
by "heart" we are to understand the intellectual appetite,
and by "flesh" the sensitive appetite."[6] All of this, of course,
is underscored by St. Thomas's central thesis that "it is the
nature of the passions to be guided by reason."[7]

The Goodness of Emotions and Feelings

When, over time, one cultivates, educates, and refines
one's feelings for what is good (first, on the natural level;
then, on the spiritual level), there is a "growing harmony
and integration that ensues" and "the emotions learn to follow reason ever more readily as they are meant to do. They
develop a habitual disposition to listen to their 'master's voice'
readily and effortlessly."[8] Furthermore, "Cultivation of the
emotional life in its entirety, not its extinction or repression,
is a prerequisite for...harmony, integration, [or] cooperation
between reason and emotions. The emotions, with their psy-
chomotor reactions (the physiological changes which accompany every emotion), exist in order to be integrated by reason;
to move man under its guidance toward the happiness for
which he is created."[9] In fact, from a Thomistic viewpoint,

this is what one would call affective maturity: the integration of reason, will, and the emotions.

Therefore, it is not by willpower alone that we are to live. Rather, the emotions *support* and *strengthen* the will in its choice of the good—when their power for affectivity has been developed. For example, when one *desires* to do something good, having that desire makes it easier to do good than if one has no "appetite" for doing good (e.g., as with being physically fit, being generous, fasting, etc.).

The development of the emotions of the concupiscible appetite (which one could also call the human or pleasure emotions) enables us not only to love what is good, but to hate what is evil; not only to desire the good, but to have an aversion to what is bad; to rejoice in the attainment of what is loved and desired, as well as to feel sad when what is hated and to be avoided becomes unavoidable. When the power for affectivity (the capacity to experience love, desire, and joy) is developed, the priest is able, for example, to empathize with others who experience difficulty, loss, and death—while offering them hope in eternal life. In fact, to spiritualize the reality of pain and suffering is to minimize it and to deny others the priest's affirmation of their experience of life.

Frankly, when St. Thomas says that the passions add to virtue (or to vice), it is clear that the passions can cause us to experience great pain or discomfort (which is not necessarily a bad or evil thing in itself). At the same time, one can imagine that, at times, the emotions vitally assist us to do what we must, either because we have been moved by something, or because through our will, we have aroused our irascible passions (our Assertive Drive) so that we have the hope and fortitude to overcome the difficulty we face. This capacity proves to be a blessing when it is fully developed through the practice of being open with one's feelings and emotions—*as well as* with one's intellect —to all that is good, true, and beautiful.

This capacity of the heart to be moved with love, desire, and joy—what we call affectivity—means that one is capable of feeling love for the goodness of things and people—of loving another for *his* own sake. This is the affirmation which is rooted in authentic *affective maturity*, when one's affectivity is guided by the highest good: the self-restraining love for another person. Here, one restrains oneself from what he desires for the sake of the *other's* good.

Moreover, this is quite different from just wanting to *help* others, which does not require one to be moved by the goodness of the person. One can help others volitionally, without the participation of the heart. Of course, such actions are still good and even virtuous, but they will not have the same effect on the person. Such actions are characterized by effectivity, or our readiness to think and act effectively, to achieve or produce something.

To illustrate the differences between effectivity and affectivity, Dr. Terruwe gives the following examples. In each is a contrast between effectivity and affectivity. First, consider the hand of a man who desires a woman; now, think of the hand of a man who desires to console a woman. Next, think of the look of a girl who is flirting; now, imagine the look of a mother toward her disabled child.[10] In the first of each of these examples, one can see the manifestation of effectivity and in the latter, affectivity. There is a stark contrast between them. What is the difference?

Affectivity produces pleasure, enjoyment, wonder, and awe; it is this attitude of receptivity which enables these emotions to exist. In contrast, effectivity *per se* does not bring feelings of joyfulness because it is focused on *producing*. Yet, when one does something in the service of what is good, one often feels happy and joyful, the fruit of effectivity in the service of affectivity. However, if this relationship is reversed, one moves toward workaholism, utilitarianism, materialism. One is caught up in restless *striving*. Living in a strictly effective manner can never bring true peace and joy. If one's attitude in life is characterized by effectivity, then his relationships will be focused on himself or a specific goal rather than on the other person. Therefore, it is very important that one's effectivity serve his affectivity.

When we protect our affectivity and what we do (that is, our effectivity) serves it, we will come not merely to *know* or *will* the good; we will also be able to be moved by and *feel* and *experience* the goodness, beauty, and truth of people, things, nature, the fine arts—as well as to feel love for God and the highest spiritual truths. Allow me to relate a personal story as an example of how this concept can manifest itself in daily life. When I was about eleven or so, I began to experience trepidation regarding the reality that the Eucharist is, indeed, the Body and Blood of Jesus Christ. I told my father about my anxiety that I would actually be eating human flesh: it was repugnant to think of it. In a very beautiful display of his affirming love for me as well as for the Lord, my father tenderly replied, "Yes, it is true that we are eating His flesh, but isn't it beautiful that because God *knew* we would not be able to receive Him if it *looked* like human flesh, instead He comes to us in *a little piece of bread.*" My father's affective response affirmed me at that tender age, and I realized that God loved me just as I was, with all my concerns. In fact, it become more apparent to me that in coming to me in the Host, God was even restraining His *own* love for me for *my* good. My father's answer also confirmed that my feelings were normal. His very brief but affirming response opened me up further to knowing God's personal love for me—that God loves me *as I am.* I had no more problems with this thought, which could have been aggravated into a fear neurosis or even scruples had I been made to feel ashamed or guilty about my thoughts and feelings. In the beautiful words of Anna Terruwe, "affectivity simultaneously brings peace and resolves difficulties."

It is often the case that people have become so effective that although they may say words of love and act in a loving way, they do not really *feel* love; therefore, the other person does not *feel* loved. Developing the habit of living affectively permits one to *receive* others as a *gift*. One might say that authentic affirmation, rooted in affectivity, is truly the "milk of human kindness."

Affectivity and the Priest

Nowadays, what we often encounter is what we deplore: the image of man as a base, animalistic creature who gives in to his passions, instincts, and lusts. All of us can agree that this is hardly affective maturity.

The opposite of this state of affairs, however, is the priest who lives only by his intellect and willpower, who appears cool-headed and rational and who can, of course, be virtuous, but who also can be distant and removed from the experiences of others. While this priest may do and achieve good things, as pastor he probably will not be experienced by his flock as a warm spiritual father. Unfortunately for his parishioners, their path to God may be diverted or delayed because of the absence of this crucial characteristic in their pastor.

Affective maturity presents a quite distinct picture. The affectively mature man, generally speaking, is someone who directs his feelings and actions reasonably but who, at the same time, is warm, available not only intellectually but emotionally, and who can readily empathize with others.

Our best model for affective maturity, naturally, is Jesus Christ. Of course, He taught the truth and knew the Scriptures. But even more than that, the context of His teaching was His affirming Presence, inasmuch as He allowed Himself to be moved with love for each person He met, thereby strengthening them to *be themselves.* For example, when the rich man came to Jesus asking for clarity about what to do with his life and possessions, and who turned away downhearted because he could not imagine giving away everything, the Scriptures say that Jesus looked at him with love.

Jesus affirmed Peter when Peter told Jesus who He was: "You are the Messiah, the Son of the living God" (Mt 16:16). Jesus said to Him, "And so I say to you, you are Peter, and upon this rock I will build my church" (Mt 16:18). Jesus emotionally loved Peter and intellectually affirmed who Peter was. Jesus did not say (as perhaps many of us would have), "when I've forgiven you for denying me three times, you'll be the rock!" Jesus *already* knew Peter was the rock.

Facing the woman caught in adultery, Jesus did not *begin* by telling her she should avoid this sin. He first protected her from stoning, called her to see herself as He knew her. He affirmed her worth by showing her she was not defined by her sin—and only *then* did He tell her to go in peace and to avoid this sin.

Jesus Himself was affirmed by God the Father. Dr. Williamson so beautifully said this in his essay: "Jesus in His human nature took courage, took strength" from the Father's words, "You are My Beloved Son."[11] The fact that we are privy to this tender exchange leads one to believe that the Father wants us to see this. Otherwise, it would not occur to us to think that Jesus would need to be strengthened. After all, He is God.

As we contemplate the Word made flesh, we might be moved by the Father's great love for us. Through the realization of His desire to redeem us, God affirmed our worth, our loveableness, our goodness. The Incarnation speaks of God's infinite, unselfish, and personal love for each of us.

Is this not the God we each long for, the God we long to encounter? This God loves us just as we are, in the midst of our sins and failings, yet *through* that very affirming love where we are *strengthened to be ourselves (our first vocation)*, He calls us to repent, to be better, to do what is right. It is His love which transforms our hearts (from the inside out) and *calls* us into relationship with Him where we *desire* to love Him and others. It is the experience of being loved *just as we are* that brings us to our knees—not as the result of force, but as the result of being drawn into His embrace. You may be who you are; and, in fact, it is for *that very reason* God loves you.

When one receives the loving gaze of the Father, one experiences a *felt* sense of his own worth—one is strengthened to be himself. Then, he "knows" his identity through intuition, which is more profound than knowing it through reason alone. The man has been strengthened in his identity because God has loved him *just as he is.*

This spiritual and emotional strengthening is authentic affirmation—it occurs when one has experienced the Father's love and desire for him in His loving *gaze.* Hence, God's love itself is the *author* of one's feelings of worth, of feeling lovable and secure.

When one has received the loving gaze of the Father, he, in turn, knows better how to be present and receptive to another person. He truly knows *how* to strengthen that person, through the authentic affirmation of that person's goodness, because he has the capacity for experiencing the *joy* of their goodness

The man who believes in and knows *this* God is very different than the man who lives on his willpower alone—who thinks, "Just do it!" is the mantra for virtuous living, who pulls up his bootstraps and *ignores* his feelings. His way of life often does not allow for the emotional connection necessary for touching or moving hearts through being attentive to the sufferings and joys of others. He is too busy doing it all himself.

Conclusion

In conclusion, the anthropology of St. Thomas Aquinas provides us with the best explanation of the integration of the passions with reason and will. It is St. Thomas who emphasizes the necessity of the passions' participation in the life of virtue (so that we may come to *love* the good with both mind and heart, or as Aquinas said, with "heart and flesh").

When the emotions are properly understood as the instruments God designed them to be under rational guidance, Christians can be free to live more spontaneously, effortlessly, honestly, and joyfully. Finally, when the priest, through his pastoral ministry, is affectively present to his parishioners, they will have the opportunity to be introduced to God's own personal love for them through the priest as their spiritual father.

NOTES

1.   Private audience of Anna Terruwe with Pope Paul VI, 1969.
2.   Paul J. Glenn, *A Tour of the Summa*, (St. Louis, MO: B. Herder Book Co.), 1960. Reference is to *Summa Theologica* Ia, IIae, q. 24, art. 3.
3.   Ibid.
4.   *The Catechism of the Catholic Church* (Washington D.C.: USCCB Publishing, 2000), sec. 1762.
5.   Conrad W. Baars, "The Christian Anthropology of Thomas Aquinas," *The Priest*, October 1974. 32.
6.   *The Catechism of the Catholic Church*, 1770; S. Th. I-II, q. 24, art.3.
7.   *Summa Theologica* I-II, q. 24, art.3.
8.   Conrad W. Baars, *The Priest*, 32.
9.   Ibid .
10.   Anna Terruwe, *Affective Relationships in the Religious Community.* Unpublished paper.
11.   See Peter S. Williamson's essay "Scriptural Foundations for the Priest as Beloved Son" in this book.

AT THE HEART OF PRIESTLY SPIRITUALITY: SONSHIP AS MISSION UNDER THE SIGN OF THE CROSS

MARGARET M. TUREK

Guided by the Christology of Hans Urs von Balthasar, I will sketch the main contours of the "filial form" of Christ's mission. I will focus upon the obediential and kenotic love of Christ, which is mobilized and sustained by His stance of contemplative intimacy toward the Father.[1] Then, I will consider some implications for the spirituality of priests and seminarians. For the latter, I depend on a fine book by Dermot Power, *A Spiritual Theology of the Priesthood*.[2] I will keep in mind the Second Vatican Council's *Decree on Priestly Training*, which sums up the full scope of the spiritual formation of priests in these few words: "Spiritual formation...should be conducted in such a way that the seminarians may learn to live in intimate and unceasing union with God the Father, through the Son Jesus Christ, in the Holy Spirit."[3]

Priesthood in Light of the Mystery of Christ

Vatican II sees the ministerial priesthood in terms of service to the Church, as continuing the ministry of Christ who loved His Bride, the Church, and gave Himself up for her.[4] In *Pastores Dabo Vobis*, St. John Paul II insists that the mission of the priest "is the *same* mission [as that] of Jesus."[5] For Balthasar, too, the mission of the priest is identified with the prolongation of Christ's presence in the Church. The ordained priesthood exists, he says, to make transparent the "inner form" of Christ's mission from the Father, to represent Christ's redemptive love for the Church for whose sake He gives Himself away.[6] This Christological vision of the priesthood grounds and animates priestly spirituality. In its light, the priest finds an *apologia* for a prayer life of interior listening and self-surrender. Here, too, the priest finds the benchmark of pastoral engagement. For Balthasar, it is a matter of seeing priesthood as Sonship given over for the Church under the sign of the Cross.[7]

The Mission of the Son

Throughout his numerous theological works, Balthasar is untiring in his efforts to trace the form or pattern of the Son's existence in mission. He discerns a Christological mission in the New Testament, already in the Synoptic tradition and also in St. Paul, which is deepened and developed in the Fourth Gospel, where John depicts Christ as He who *is* "the One *Sent*": Christ *is* the Son sent into the world by the Father.[8] And this means that Christ's identity as the Beloved Son is thoroughly expressed in His mission from the Father.

Obedience as the Inner Form of the Son's Mission

The inner disposition that shapes the Son's whole existence in mission is obedience, His obedient love for the Father who sends Him. Obedient love marks the Son's entire path, from the generative bosom of the eternal Father, to the virginal womb of Mary unto the Cross on Golgotha.[9] "I came down from heaven...[to do] the will of the one who sent me" (Jn 6:38); "[T]he world must know that I love the Father and I do just as the Father has commanded me (Jn14:31); "I always do what is pleasing to him" (Jn 8:29). Indeed, the mission of the Son is the way of filial love in obedience. The Son's fundamental stance as "the One sent" consists in the receptive readiness to let Himself be disposed of by the Father, in His complete availability to accomplish the will of the Father.[10]

Obedience as the Human Expression of the Son's Divine Love in the Trinity

The concept of mission (the mission *of the Son*) straightaway leads us to uncover its inner-divine Trinitarian depths. In agreement with St. Thomas, Balthasar regards the historical mission of the Son as the graciously free translation or expression of His eternal generation from the Father. This insight brings Balthasar to conclude that since obedience is the "inner form" of the mission of the Son, then a divine "supra-form" analogous to obedience denotes His eternal Sonship. Obedience is the proper *human* expression of the Son's *divine* love for the Father within the Trinity. It is the revelation in *human* terms of the Son's *divine* and *eternal* self-surrender to the Father.[11] Hence, it has nothing of servile fear or groveling subservience about it. Rather, it is "grounded in [and reflects] the *filial* way in which the Son possesses the one divine will with the Father and the Spirit."[12]

The Sonship of Christ and the Priesthood of Christ

As Balthasar traces the contours of the mission of Christ, he consistently draws out its "twin dimensions": as the obedient Son, Christ willingly *surrenders Himself* into the Father's hands so that the *Father* may *give Him* for the salvation of the world. These "twin dimensions" of Christ's filial mission frame Balthasar's depiction of Christ as both *priest* and *victim*. Inasmuch as the Son turns toward the Father in readiness to surrender all that He is and has, He is the prototype of the *priest*: one who *offers* up gifts to God. Inasmuch as the Son surrenders *Himself* to the *Father's* disposal, He is "a *victim* to be sacrificed."[13] The Son serves as both Priest and Victim because His pattern of relating to the Father is a unity of these two aspects: He both *offers* Himself to the Father and lets Himself *be offered by* the Father. As Priest, the Son *gives* Himself up (see Heb 3:14); as the Lamb of God, He lets Himself *be given* up (see Jn 1:28).[14] In Balthasar's words: For the Son, "[t]his gift of self is only an *act* in the sense of being a *consent* to be delivered. This has to be seen in a Trinitarian context. The whole [Trinitarian] action [for us] is contained within the love of the Father who *gives* him up and the love of the Son who lets himself be disposed of."[15] Moreover, as we have seen, this unity of *self-giving* and allowing Himself *to be given* does not make its first appearance at the Son's final "hour." Rather, it is present throughout the entire span of the Son's earthly life. Indeed, Christ's priesthood is intrinsic to the way in which His Sonship is expressed in mission, precisely because priesthood's inner form has its source and norm in Sonship. Priesthood is synonymous with Sonship, says Balthasar, insofar as its inner shape is derived from the Son's obedient love which makes His entire mission an existential self-offering, a perfect sacrifice.[16]

Kenosis: the Form of the Self-Giving of the Son

The Christological *hymn* in *Philippians* (2:6-11) offers us further insight into the dynamic form of the Son's existence in mission. Filial obedience is from first to last an emptying of Himself to the end that *another*, the *Father*, be glorified through Him. According to Balthasar's reading of this hymn, the Son's consent to being sent and His attendant self-emptying are an exegesis of His *divine* love for the Father and, thus, also of the Trinity's eternal life of *caritas*.

Following Mikhail Bulgakov, Balthasar regards the Father's eternal initiative of self-giving as the *"original kenosis"* of absolute love. For it is premierly the Father who, in begetting the Son as "God from God," does not grasp the divinity to Himself but empties Himself without remainder. The Father does not give merely a portion of the divinity, but hands over to the Son *all* that is His, the divinity in its entirety. Nor does He exist as the first divine person "before" this kenotic self-surrender, as if in a prior disposition of conserving for Himself the wealth of the divinity. Rather, the Father *"is* this original movement of self-giving that holds nothing back."[17] To be sure, the Father surrenders His divine substance in such a manner that, as He gives it over to the Son, He, nevertheless, retains it at the same time; otherwise, He would really cease to be God (see Fourth Lateran Synod, DS 805). And as for the Son, the divinity He receives from the Father is originally shaped by the Father to the form and measure of emptying oneself of all for the sake of the other.[18] In the words of Balthasar:

> Only in holding-onto-nothing-for-himself is God *Father*; he pours forth his substance and generates the Son; and only in holding-onto-nothing-for-himself of what has been received does the Son show himself to be of the same essence of the Father, and only in this shared holding-onto-nothing-for-themselves are they one in the Spirit, who is…the eternal product of this ceaselessly flowing movement of self-surrender…. If the Second Person steps out of this circling life in order to offer the world what is the totality of God, his style of life will not be the grasping demeanor of a pantocrator but the opposite: *the Son lays bare the heart of the Father* as he becomes the servant of all and breathes out into the world his Spirit of service and of the last place.[19]

The kenotic form, then, of the Son's existence in mission, His self-renunciation and His being-for-others, is rightly seen as the definitive translation of His Beloved Sonship, and *for this very reason*, as the consummate revelation of God's Fatherhood. To live authentically, the mission of Sonship involves a self-emptying that permits a pure transparency between the One Sent and the One Who Sends. Christ can readily assure Philip (and us, as well) that to see Him is to see the Father, since He lives out a filial asceticism which effectively detaches Him from any desire to think or act "on His own," or to set His own terms. Assuredly, Christ's perfect self-*de*tachment is but the flipside of his single-hearted *at*tachment to the will of his heavenly Father. He is passionately invested in His role as the Father's representative, such that every note of self-renunciation, in fact, signals His heart's desire to go to whatever lengths the Father's "ordinance of love"[20] determines for Him.

But now, *how* is Christ's passionate self-investment mobilized and sustained?

The Unity of Contemplation and Action in Christ

In agreement with the entire New Testament, Balthasar perceives that the Son's mission unfolds both as an expression of the Father's love and as His own unfailing response to that love. The Fourth Gospel bears this out in numerous passages, perhaps most notably in John 5:19-20: "a son cannot do anything on his own, but only what he sees his father doing; for what he does, his son will do also. For the Father loves his Son and shows him everything that he himself does." This suggests that the Son's *active* self-investment in His mission from the Father has its roots in His *contemplation* of the Father and, more precisely, in His contemplation of the Father's *action*. What Christ "sees" in contemplating the Father is the God who shows Himself to be love in action, the God who so loves the world that He *gives* His only Son (see Jn 3:16). And in "seeing" the Father's love in action, Christ is induced to willingly do likewise, to give *Himself* over for the sake of the world. Christ's original stance *vis-à-vis* the Father is a contemplative one. But this should not be mistaken for a purely passive stance. Rather, it is a stance of active receptivity. Christ stands as ever ready to mirror the Father's action which He contemplates, ever ready to receive and actualize the Father's will on behalf of the world. As we have noted, Balthasar repeatedly describes Christ's inner stance in such terms: as a constant readiness to obey His heavenly Father.[21]

Sonship is lived out to perfection by Christ precisely in this form: one that combines the greatest contemplative receptivity to the Father's will and the greatest active readiness to accomplish it.[22]

Moreover, this stance which the Son exhibits throughout His earthly life reaches its zenith, its definitive and unsurpassable form, in His Passion and Death on the Cross. Christ "sees" that the Father, in giving over His Son, is the *first* to commit Himself to the path of self-sacrifice. For in giving over His Son to us sinners, the Father gives all that His paternal heart has to live on, so to speak. It is this love shown by the Father—this sacrifice of His *paternal* heart—that draws the Son to Calvary and serves Him as the model that He imitates in allowing the lance to pierce His own Sacred Heart.[23]

Obedience and Priesthood

How does the priest live Christ's own filial obedience? The call to the ministerial priesthood is a call to share in Christ's beloved Sonship. Christ's Sonship, moreover, is expressed in "Christ's obediential stance before the Father, which constitutes the very heart of his Priesthood."[24] Obedience, therefore, is essential to the purpose of the priesthood as an official representation of the *filial* love of Christ, the Eternal High Priest. In other words, the priest's obedience is a condition of his ecclesial mission to be transparent to the Son, to serve as an *alter Christus*. It entails an unreserved giving of self which takes the form of letting himself be given over to his pastoral mission. Indeed, Balthasar suggests that the clearest evidence for the continuing influence of Christ on His priests is found in their willingness to yield themselves to God's will, allowing the Father to dispose of them for the good of the Church. This means that the priest's participation in Christ's own priestly and pastoral mission involves a self-donation that is at once both deeply personal and pastoral.[25]

Now, in order to foster that *subjective* assimilation to Christ which priestly configuration entails, the priest is called to an obedience that takes *objective*, concrete shape within the hierarchical structure of the Church.[26] "The priest, at his ordination, promises obedience to his Bishop" and, thereby, makes himself available to the pastoral needs of the local Church as discerned by ecclesiastical authority.[27] St. John Paul II, in *Pastores Dabo Vobis*, is careful to keep the personal and the ecclesial, or the subjective and the objective dimensions of priestly obedience, closely linked together. The priest's exercise of pastoral ministry can never be reduced to what is personally preferable or convenient. Rather, it is to be exercised on the basis of a filial and obediential relationship with his Bishop which is directed toward the building up of the Church.[28] In the words of St. John Paul II:

> This "submission" to those invested with ecclesial authority is in no way a kind of humiliation. It flows instead from the responsible freedom of the priest who accepts not only the demands of an organized and organic ecclesial life, but also that grace of discernment and responsibility in ecclesial decisions which was assured by Jesus to his Apostles and their successors, for the sake of faithfully safeguarding the mystery of the Church and serving the structure of the Christian community along its common path toward salvation.[29]

Moreover, the *obedience* asked of a priest is meant to serve as a basis of the ecclesial *authority* that he represents and exercises regarding the parish community. As St. John Paul II observes: "Only the person who knows how to obey in Christ is really able to require obedience from others in accordance with the Gospel."[30]

Balthasar's reflections move along similar lines. The *authority* represented by the priest is that of Christ, the beloved Son, who was *obedient* unto death. Hence, it is an *authority* which, as it summons others to *obedience*, presents itself as a model to be imitated. Christ incorporates the priest ever more deeply into His own filial obedience in order that He may entrust to the priest participation in the responsibility of the Good Shepherd, who gives His life for His sheep (Jn 10:15). For what Christ expects from the priest on whom He confers His pastoral authority is this: as Christ "laid down his life for us," so, too, the priest will "lay down [his life] for [his] brothers" (1 Jn 3:16).[31] The *obedient* availability for pastoral service which informs the priest's exercise of *authority* is, therefore, a condition that allows the heart of the Good Shepherd to shine through with greater transparency. What St. John Paul II and Balthasar are leading us to see is that obedience should be placed "at the very pivot of the efficacy of ecclesial ministry."[32] This is true, in the first place, of the efficacy of *Christ's* ministry. "In accordance with St. Paul's words to the Christians at Philippi, the priest should have 'the mind which was in Christ Jesus,'"[33] whose exaltation to an unlimited share in the Father's lordship and authority hinges on His unlimited obedience, even to Death on a Cross.

Furthermore, both facets (being obedient and being granted authority) are directed to and culminate in the glorification of God the *Father*. To be sure, there are many layers of meaning to be explored and more than one approach to take in meditating on this pre-Pauline hymn. But let us follow Balthasar along one route. He observes that Christ, by His loving *obedience*, reveals the *authority* of the Father—and, hence, shows us the archetype of every (derived) authority in heaven and on earth (see Eph 3:14-15). Christ's assenting self-surrender is the flawless mirror in which the Father's authority can be seen as a modality of utterly selfless, other-directed love. The Gospels plainly witness to the fact that, in the mission of Christ, there is present the continuous personal guidance of the Father that shapes Christ's decisions. This shaping, however, never resorts to *over*powering Christ's human will. Quite the opposite. Far from *over*powering the human freedom of Christ to make Him submissive, the Father *em*powers His freedom to be obedient in all things.

Once again, Balthasar points to John 5:19-20 as indicating *how* this empowerment takes place: the Father shows the Son "everything that he himself does," shows the Son the *way* in which he *himself* exercises authority—namely, as expressive of an altruistic and uncalculatingly generous love—which wills to serve the needs of all (Mk 10:43-44). Christ, in beholding the manner in which the Father exercises authority, is moved to entrust Himself to the Father's will. The Father to whom Christ can say in the garden of Gethsemane, "not my will but yours be done," (Lk 22:42) is the Father whom He has always known to be utterly selfless and steadfast in His love. Christ's obedience, then, is not merely external compliance with a command, but rather, an interior response to known love. And when Christ, in turn, exercises the authority He receives from the Father (see Mt 28:18; Phil 2:10-11), He exemplifies a pattern that "completely undermines relationships of domination" and coercion.[34]

If *Ephesians* defines the proper exercise of authority according to the example of Christ who "handed himself over" (Eph 5:25) for His beloved, the *Johannine Gospel* emphasizes the evocative efficacy (the power to call forth obedience) that resides in the *manner* in which authority is exercised. Christ issues commands to His Apostles as their master and teacher only after modeling for them the way He knows the Father to act in authority. "As the Father loves . . . , so *I* also love . . . " [emphasis added] (Jn 15:9); "If *I*, therefore, . . . have washed your feet, you ought to wash . . .. [A]s *I* have done for you, you should also do" [emphasis added] (Jn 13:14-15). Thus, for John, it is true premierly of God the Father that exhibiting the disposition of unreserved giving of self for the benefit of the Beloved is integral to the engendering of the obediential response.[35] This remains the case for the ecclesial authority conferred on the priest. Balthasar regards it as meant to lead the faithful, gently but persistently, beyond the many ego-entanglements which constrain our freedom, to an inner spontaneity of filial obedience. The priest, who is himself obedient, draws the faithful beyond servile fear to love's "fearlessness" (see 1 Jn 4:18). The more a priest assimilates the *obedience* of the Son, the more efficacious will be his exercise of *authority* in evoking obedience from the people of God.

Kenosis and Priesthood

As we previously noted in reference to Phil 2:6-11, the "filial form" of Christ's mission is, from first to last, an emptying of Himself. Now, since the priest participates in the mission of Christ and its continuation in the Church, he finds the origin and norm of his spiritual life and ministry in the *kenosis* of Christ.[36] In order to conform himself to Christ's kenotic love, the priest should look to the opening of the pierced heart of the Son and see that he, too, is called to surrender what is most intimate and personal for the benefit of the community. In Balthasar's words:

> The priest, who by reason of his office is the bearer of Christ's grace, can find no other and no better answer to this grace than to be subjectively the kind of priest that Christ wants him to be, that is, ... a priest who offers his whole life as a holocaust in the service of God and [the Church]. No priestly [spirituality] can have any other basic content than the total expropriation of one's own private interests...so that one may be a pure instrument for the accomplishment of Christ's designs for the Church. [The grace to make such a gift] is conferred on the priest with the gift of sacramental grace and the indelible mark of his priesthood.[37]

St. John Paul II says something akin to this in *Pastores Dabo Vobis*. Christ brings:

> his pastoral charity to perfection on the Cross with a complete exterior and interior an *emptying* of self, [which] is both the model and source of the virtues of obedience, chastity and poverty which the priest is called to live out as an expression of his pastoral charity for his brothers and sisters. In accordance with St Paul's words to the Christians at Philippi, the priest should have "the mind which was in Christ Jesus," *emptying* himself of his own "self" so as to discover...the royal road of union with God and unity with his brothers and sisters (cf. Phil 2:5).[38]

Ruled out, then, is any attitude toward the gift of priesthood that suggests self-entitlement or self-promotion. Far from being a gift to be grasped, clutched at, or fashioned to suit oneself, it is meant to draw the priest into the Christological depths of a wholehearted self-renunciation. This self-renunciation, moreover, should be discernible in those who are consecrated to speak and act *in persona Christi*. Indeed, just as Christ came to reveal and glorify, not Himself, but the Father, so, too, the priest is called to direct attention away from himself and toward someone else, toward Christ. This "comes to its crystallization," says Power (following Balthasar):

> in the liturgical office of the priest, [inasmuch as] the priest is called to speak, not of himself nor for himself, nor to act by his own strength, but to stand in the place of another—to become an *alter Christus*. The words "This is my body" and "I absolve you"… reveal the depth of involvement *with Christ* to which priesthood is drawn. [The depth of Christ's Eucharistic love is to unfold in the life of the priest:] like Christ, he is to be taken and blessed, broken and given, and not only in terms of liturgical gesture, but also in the concrete practice of loving the community.[39]

The Unity of Contemplation and Action in Priesthood

If the priest's pastoral mission is to be fully realized, he needs to empty himself to make room for the will of the Father. What this amounts to is that the mission of the priest requires that he be a contemplative-in-action in imitation of Christ who is the pre-eminent contemplative-in-action. For, as we observed earlier, Christ's stance of obedience combines contemplative openness to the Father with active readiness to answer the Father. The Father shows Himself to Christ as the archetype of infinite love who is to be reflected in the Son's obedient action as man.

Christ, on His side, turns toward the Father in a stance of active receptivity. And in "seeing" the *Father's* self-outpouring in love, He is moved to respond by disposing of *Himself* in imitation of the Father. "As the Father loves me," says Christ, "so I also love you" (Jn 15:9). In this light, we can better understand what Balthasar means when he says of Christ: "to be a Child of the Father holds primacy over the whole drama of salvation.... [T]he total redemptive deed with its emphatically 'adult' earnestness can, in the last analysis, be accomplished only by virtue of the childlike stance," the contemplative, mirroring stance of the Son-of-God-made-man.[40] Just so, the priest needs to practice contemplative prayer, since it is a springboard to a Christ-like availability to the will and work of God.

However, if Christ enjoyed unparalleled contemplative knowledge of the Father as the motivating force of His obedient action, does not this place the priest at a real disadvantage?

What needs to be recognized is that the Son, precisely through His obedient action, is the unparalleled revealer of the Father. It is because the Father shows the Son everything He does that the Son is incited to do likewise, and in so doing, the Son shows us the Father (coupling Jn 5:19-20 with 14:9-11). As Balthasar points out: "[w]hat we are looking at when we contemplate the love of God is '*Christ giving himself in love.*'"[41] And in contemplating this, God's active involvement with the world in Christ (above all, in Christ Crucified), the priest is spurred, mobilized to live his priesthood as a total gift of self.

Accordingly, Balthasar situates priesthood between two poles which he variously identifies as interiority and mission, discipleship and apostolate, or contemplation and action. For him, it is not to be doubted that a certain primacy belongs to personal discipleship, or to contemplative interiority, which engenders the momentum of pastoral service. Of course, interiority is not to be confused with a narrowly individualistic, self-preoccupied disposition. Rather, at issue here is an interiority that participates in and is shaped by the inner form of divine Sonship; and, thus, it is an interiority ordered toward *caritas*, love of another. Precisely *this* kind of interiority grounds the priest's ministry in the very depths of the most holy Trinity.[42]

Final Remarks

In this essay, I have illustrated how Balthasar integrates theology and spirituality, how he places Catholic doctrine in the service of God's work of ongoing conversion and transformation in Christ. Here is a theology that begins with a contemplative beholding of the incarnate Son, and aims not only to heal the eyes of our hearts to "see" God, but also—and inseparably—to draw us to collaborate with God in the formation of saints . . . and of saintly priests.

NOTES

1. I have incorporated ideas found in my extended study of Balthasar's Trinitarian theology, *Towards a Theology of God the Father: Hans Urs von Balthasar's Theodramatic Approach* (Bern, Switzerland: Peter Lang Publishing, Inc., 2001), as well as in my article, "'As the Father Has Loved Me' (Jn 15:9): Balthasar's Theodramatic Approach to a Theology of God the Father," *Communio: International Catholic Review* 26 (1999), 295-318.

2. See Dermot Power, *A Spiritual Theology of the Priesthood: The Mystery of Christ and the Mission of the Priest* (Washington D.C.: The Catholic University of America Press, 1998).

3. Paul VI, *Optatam Totius* (1965), sec. 8.

4. See Kenan B. Osborne, O.F.M., *Priesthood: A History of the Ordained Ministry in the Roman Catholic Church* (New York: Paulist Press, 1988) 3-29; and Power, 14-15.

5. John Paul II, *Pastores Dabo Vobis* (1992), sec. 14.

6. See Power, 19.

7. See Power, 48.

8. See Power, 34-35.

9. See Balthasar, *The Threefold Garland* (San Francisco: Ignatius Press, 1982) 30.

10. See Balthasar, *Theo-drama III: Dramatis Personae: The Person of Christ* (San Francisco: Ignatius Press, 1992), 39, 160, 186, 522. In addition, see Turek, *Towards a Theology of God the Father*, 48. See also Thomas G. Dalzell, *The Dramatic Encounter of Divine and Human Freedom in the Theology of Hans Urs von Balthasar* (Bern, Switzerland: Peter Lang Publishing, Inc., 2000), 158.

11. See Balthasar, *Theo-drama III*, 22, 187, 530; *Threefold Garland*, 31; and *The Christian State of Life* (San Francisco: Ignatius Press, 1983), 78. In addition see Turek, *Towards a Theology of God the Father*, 49.

12. Power, 36.

13. Balthasar, *Christian State of Life*, 252.

14. See Balthasar, *Christian State of Life*, 252-53; and Power 32 and 45.

15. Balthasar, *Christian State of Life* (German edition) 257, cited by Power, 46.

16. See Power, 36 and 46.

17. Balthasar, *Theo-drama IV: The Action* (San Francisco: Ignatius Press, 1994), 323.

18. See Turek, *Towards a Theology of God the Father*, 106 and 109.

19. Balthasar, *Pneuma und Institution* (Einsiedeln, 1974), 114f.

20. Balthasar, *Unless You Become Like This Child* (San Francisco: Ignatius Press, 1991) 31.

21.   See Balthasar, *Threefold Garland*, 32; and Turek, *Towards a Theology of God the Father*, 55.

22.   See Dalzell, 157-59 and 215.

23.   See Turek, *Towards a Theology of God the Father*, 117-19. Jean Galot, S.J., offers reflections that are compatible with Balthasar's. See Galot's *Abba, Father: We Long to See Your Face* (New York: Alba House, 1997), 134-38.

24.   Power, 103.

25.   See Power, 100.

26.   See Power, 101.

27.   Power, 101-102.

28.   See Power, 102.

29.   *Pastores Dabo Vobis*, sec. 28.

30.   *Pastores Dabo Vobis*, sec. 28; cited by Power, 102.

31.   Balthasar, *Christian State of Life*, 268.

32.   Power, 103.

33.   *Pastores Dabo Vobis*, sec. 28.

34.   Power, 98.

35.   See Turek, *Towards a Theology of God the Father*, 108-109.

36.   See Power, 3, 49, 54, 98.

37.   Balthasar, *Christian State of Life*, 275.

38.   *Pastores Dabo Vobis*, sec. 81; cited in Power, 105.

39.   Power, 48.

40.   Balthasar, *Unless You Become*, 63-4.

41.   Balthasar, *Engagement with God* (San Francisco: Ignatius Press, 2008), 47. My italics.

42.   See Power, 79 and 129.

SEEING THE EUCHARIST, SEEING THE FATHER

DAVID VINCENT MECONI, S.J.

Each of us knows all too well that none of us is receptive enough to live the Christian life as God's own beloved; none of us is strong and consistent enough to live the Christian life in joyful obedience. None of us is able to live the life of Christ's priest; *but Jesus is*—and He longs these days and forever to give us His own life to live, to extend His own life to each of us. We are to be more than mere voyeurs of the Christian life, lazy bystanders who glance every now and then at what Christ is doing. His entire life is for us, not only to believe in or to gaze upon, but to become. For this purpose alone, He continues to incarnate Himself in this world and continues to send the Holy Spirit of sanctifying union. The Church, thus, was founded not to establish a new religion but to communicate a *new and unmatchable relationship*, a new love between God and humanity, our acceptance as sons and daughters by the same Father as Jesus Christ Himself.

This essay discusses the way that we can approach the theme of beloved sonship by directing our thoughts toward the Eucharist as the way to the Father. When Pope Benedict

XVI (in his first volume of *Jesus of Nazareth*) suggests that
the entire Christian mystery is contained in one word, Father,
Abba, we are reminded that all of our theology, prayer, and
preaching must be explicitly contextualized in the Trinitarian
life who is our God: "This one word [Father] contains the
whole history of redemption."[1] For to receive the Christ is
to be caught up into Christ's own oblation before the Father
in the Spirit. Our faith is ultimately about being transformed
by personal relationships. "All of us, gazing with unveiled
face on the glory of the Lord, are being transformed into the
same image from glory to glory" (2 Cor 3:18).

We have been made in the image and likeness of God so
that we might have a relationship with Him. "Then God
said: Let us make human beings in our image, after our likeness. . . . God created mankind in his image; in the image
of God he created them" (Gn 1:26-27). This primal biblical
truth was recast by Vatican II into the call to become gift:
"This likeness reveals that man, who is the only creature on
earth which God willed for itself, cannot fully find himself
except through a sincere gift of himself." [2] How different is
this understanding of the relationship between divine and
human persons than found in the Hellenic culture in which
God Himself took flesh.

Recall the three inscriptions found inscribed at the Temple at Delphi: (1) "Know thyself" (γνῶθι σεαυτόν), (2) "Nothing in excess" (μηδέν ἄγαν), and (3) "Commitment brings mis-
fortune" (Εγγύα πάρα δ'ἄτη). Each maxim equates the virtuous
man with one who is in control of his passions by removing
himself from human engagement and personal interaction.
Christianity, however, insists not only on a God who is
eternally constituted by relationship but also on a savior who

becomes human, thus identifying His own self with every human soul. That image is unlike the Greek image of a god whose strength is marked by his ability to remain aloof from personal dependency and whose success is measured by his imperviousness and inability to be changed by the vicissitudes of humanity. The God of Christianity is one whose very life is to live unto the Father in the Spirit and whose very mission is to pour His own life out only to be received and accepted by mere creatures.

Here, then, I would like to offer three movements the Eucharist invites: (1) a movement upward as son to the Father, (2) a movement outward as brothers and sisters to one another, and (3) a movement inward as the beloved whose own mystery calls out for wholeness. For each of these movements, the Trinity is our model and pattern. Remember, our God is one whose very self is constituted by relationship. Whereas the human person is constituted only partially by his or her relationships with others (for example, my father has died; I still remain), each Divine Person is essentially, wholly, constituted by the other. You and I have all had friends and teachers come in and out of our lives, but we remain essentially who we are. That is not the way in God: the Father does not have His own self-possessed divinity separate from the Son and the Spirit. There is no "autonomy" in God because the identity of each person is intelligible only in relationship. I used to think this autonomy of humanity was a blessing, a protection against anyone getting too close, against becoming too dependent on the person and the presence of another. In the words of Capuchin Father Thomas Weinandy:

For human beings not to be completely constituted by

their relationships may first appear to be a good thing.
Human persons possess an independent integrity apart
from their relationships. However, it is precisely this
independent integrity which does not allow a human
person to be given completely to another, but he or
she must do so only through mediating words (words
of kindness and love) and actions (hugs, kisses, sexual
relations, etc.) which express only a partial giving of
oneself even if one's intention is to give the whole of
oneself. This is not the case with the Trinity.

The persons of the Trinity are eternally constituted in
their own singular identity only in relation to one another,
and thus they subsist as who they are only within their
mutual relationships. In their relationships to one another
each person of the Trinity subsistently defines, and is
equally subsistently defined by, the other persons. Thus
the persons of the Trinity are subsistent relations.[3]

There is no human relationship that completely constitutes any of us; we (especially as Americans) possess an
autonomy that, at first blush, seems to be a sort of hidden
perfection: "No one can ever get to me that much; no one
can ever have too much of a claim on me." Yet, it is precisely
this self-sufficiency that does not allow us to imitate the Trinity fully. Whereas the Son is wholly reliant upon the Father to
be Son, and the Father is entirely constituted as Father only
in relationship to the Son and the Spirit conjoining and, thus,
altogether dependent upon both Father and Son to be Union,
you and I are only partially determined by the presence of
another. As we grow in holiness, however, as we grow in
imitation of the Triune Love and instead of becoming more

autonomous, more independent, we instead become more aware of others, more open toward others, more vulnerable, more docile to the Spirit, more *disponible* as God's own children.

Recently, Fr. Dick Tomasek, S.J. died on the feast of the Transfiguration. He bequeathed to me all his (unpublished) diaries and journals. In one most insightful entry, he writes:

> As the baptized, as the ordained, it is especially essential to know and claim this dual life: in the world but not of it, a citizen of heaven but still a wayfarer on earth, a priest of Christ but still a man tempted to sin. It is important to know that in every limit and emptiness and darkness of this present kenotic phase of my earthly life in Jesus and his life in me, there is precisely the limitless, and full light of the resurrected and ascended life which is mine by grace.

Another way of saying this is that in his seeming absence is his presence: in his crucifixion and resurrection, in his union with the Father and with every human soul, in his self-emptying and consequent self-giving. And so it is with me, with us. The Paschal Mystery of union with the Trinity, with the Three Self-given and Self-emptied Persons who are subsistently related to each other, so I too want to be: a relation from God, to God and in God. Therefore, in each moment, in each sacrament of the present moment, I am embraced by him and I embrace him in precisely the concrete circumstances of my earthly life.

As made in the image and likeness of the living community of divine love, Trinitarian relations must, therefore, become both the model and goal of our own lives and especially of our own priestly service to God's people, a people who (perhaps, unknowingly) also cry out to be known, to be loved, and to see themselves in another.

Toward this end, the Lord instituted His Holy Eucharist. The night before He handed Himself over to the isolating powers of sin and death, He handed Himself over first to the Church's sacramental worship, thereby continuing His incarnate presence for all time. (This is now my body. This is now my blood . . . broken and poured out for you . . . raised and transformed in you!) Here, we, too, see our movement upward to the Father enabled and effected by the Son's great exchange, our movement outward to our brothers and sisters, and our journeys inward as we come to see who we are before the One who has become us.

Upward as Sons and Daughters

As the Son's immanent and eternal stance is always one before the Father, the Beloved receiving the Lover, His role in the economy is, likewise, to show us the Father—to create in us that same receptivity in welcoming the Father. The Son, thus, becomes the space in each baptized soul where the Father is enabled to pour out His own life, His own attributes, His own nature. It is here we come to see ourselves as adopted children, sharing the same filiality of the Son's nature through grace.

There are three ways to come before the Father: (1) as the *natus*-God, the only begotten Son, (2) as the *datus*-God, the Spirit who is the gift of God, and (3) as the *factus*-god, the one made into a child of God through grace. One Son is not enough for such a perfectly loving Father; He wants a myriad of sons and daughters, so in His Son, He adopts all willing to come to Him. The Nicene Fathers hinted at this concept when they qualified our belief in the Son as one "begotten, not made," in that there are, thus, some sons and daughters who are, in fact, "made" so. At the altar, we see our new status as sons and daughters: no longer slaves obedient so as to escape punishment, no longer soldiers who execute orders only to be repaid, but sons and daughters who now gather freely, who are now fed on the bread of angels, children who live only to hand their own lives over to their Father and family. If we so consent to being caught up in the Son's eternal oblation to the Father, our entire lives are transformed. Only here are we released from the self-imposed prisons we, ironically, find more appealing than the freedom offered by discipleship. This transformation is the act of deification, an audacious term brought about by the Son's becoming human, our becoming God. Divinization is ultimately an ecclesial process where we avail ourselves of the life of the God-man so as to appropriate His own life into ours: every prayer, every Mass, every confession, every Hour of Adoration must have this purpose as its final end, to become Christ!

The Lord has come to fulfill the Law by removing from us our illusory autonomy, to open our "I" into a "we," to remove all of our sniggling "mine's" and "my's" and amplify our understanding of "self" into essential relationship: in Christ, we are called to let go of our illusions of self-dependency and isolation, to see that our only true life, our only lasting goodness, consists in becoming sharers in the Divine life. We are, thus, called to let go of being "merely human," to rise above our own fallen passions and instincts, so as to be willing to be elevated into something more alive, something forever flourishing. When that happens, we begin no longer to do things *for* Christ or even *with* Christ; but we begin to see our ministry, our prayer, our recreation as ways we *are* Christ: to teach and to preach *as* Christ. "Therefore, let us rejoice and give thanks, not only that we have been made Christians but that we have been made Christ (*Ergo gratulemur et agamus gratias: non solum christianos esse, sed Christum*) . . . We have been made Christ. For if he is the head, we are the members—a whole man, he and we."[4] In Christ, our humanity no longer simply belongs to us; we have been claimed, consecrated, Christified. In taking on the fullness of humanity, the Word invites each human to transfer his or her own self over into the one in whose image each has been made. Only here are all contraries reconciled: sinner and saint, divinity and humanity. The infinite is now known through the finite; immortality, through death; sovereignty, through service.

Only with the Son in our midst are we enabled to pray the Lord's prayer; only after the consecration of merely natural elements are we ready to lay claim to this new status as sons and daughters. For, on the natural level, we could continue uttering "I" and "my"; but now, in Christ, we are widened so as to pray "Our." While, on the natural level, our biological father may be "Jack," or "Ed," here, in this Church, the first person of the Almighty Trinity reveals himself as "Abba," as our Father. Yet, C.S. Lewis asks us:

> Do you now see what those words ["Our Father"] mean?
> They mean quite frankly, that you are putting yourself
> in the place of a son of God. To put it bluntly, you are
> dressing up as Christ. If you like, you are pretending.
> Because, of course, the moment you realise what the

words mean, you realise that you are not a son of God.
. . . So that, in a way, this dressing up as Christ is a piece
of outrageous cheek. But the odd thing is that He has
ordered us to do it.[5]

Our Eucharistic life must, thus, be not only the realization
of our divine adoption but its appropriation, as well, as this is
the entire hope of the Lord's instituting this continuation of
His Incarnation, that the whole of creation can be "presented
to the Father through the death and the Resurrection of
Christ. Through Christ the Church can offer the sacrifice of
praise in thanksgiving for all that God has made good, beautiful, and just in creation and in humanity."[6]

Far from removing us from the goodness of God's good
creation, the Eucharist immerses us back into the world
where God Himself incarnates Himself. The Host instructs
God's children how He saved the world, not from heaven
and not as spirit, but by entering into this created order with
all the humanity you and I often ignore, take for granted, or
worst, snub and exploit. Our flesh and blood, our relationships, our learning, our sexuality, our endeavors, and our
experiences are precisely the means by which God elevates
earth to heaven, humanity becoming the fulcrum upon which
all is lifted and loved. If that is so, we begin to see how cel-
ebration and adoration must also include service and the new
mandate to love one another, to wash each other clean.

Unconvinced of the Father's love for us, we remain cold
and aloof; unwilling to receive the Father's own pledge of our
worth and eternal significance, we instead find ourselves petty
and short with others–always feeling alone, always feeling
uninvited, not worthy of perfection, unable to know joy. The

love of neighbor is founded on the love of self, of course; and it is our own appropriation as beloved sons and daughters that impels us outward to the rest of God's people.

Outward as Brothers and Sisters

The *Catechism of the Catholic Church*, therefore, holds before us how: "The Eucharist commits us to the poor. To receive in truth the Body and Blood of Christ given up for us, we must recognize Christ in the poorest, his brethren. . . ."[7] And, quoting Chrysostom: "You have tasted the Body of the Lord, yet you do not recognize your brother . . . you dishonor this table when you do not judge worthy of sharing your food someone judged worthy to take part in this meal. . . . God freed you from all your sins and invited you here, but you have not become more merciful."[8]

From the Church's beginnings, Apostles and Church Fathers have maintained that this new way of knowing and serving God is not a religion of achievement but of relationship. Even the Son of God lives a public life, not for His own self but for the salvation of human persons and the glory of His Father in heaven. As you gaze upon the Host, as you elevate the Host in your own priestly hands, see how all of God's people are here merged, here united. As at the Incarnation, the Son of God assumed all humanity into Himself, thus elevating His body, the Church, to the Father, you too are to gather all men and women, especially those for whom our Lord has a special love—the distressed and poor, the unchurched and the wanting—and bring them to the Father, to become for them the Good Shepherd who leaves the ninety-nine, leaves those with whom you agree and have natural affinity, to pursue those who have turned from the flock.

St. John Chrysostom challenges each of us still:

> Do you wish to pay honor to the Savior's body? Refuse to neglect it when you see it naked. Refuse to honor his body in Church with silk vestments while outside you dismiss his body numb, cold, and naked. For the same one who said, "This is my body" is the same one who said, "You saw me hungry and you gave me no food. As you did it not to one of the least of my brothers and sisters, you did it not to me." Honor him, my brothers and sisters, by sharing what you have with the poor. For what God needs is not golden chalices, but golden souls.[9]

A true priest never pits Liturgy against charity, propriety over transparency, a rubrical facade over a heartfelt response. God has become a man and is found not only in the Jesus of Nazareth 2000 years ago but in every Host into which He has drained His life, in every chalice into which He has poured His very lifeblood, but also in His people, the *corpus mysticum* which we often find burdensome and unable to control.

There is a solid theological tradition of stating this concept in a rather shocking and, perhaps, startling way: Christ has three bodies! It seems to have begun with how Origen united the first body of Christ, His biological body, the *soma typikon*, with the Eucharist, which then overflows into His mystical body, the *ecclesia soma*, the Church. Here is the the *corpus triforme* of Amalarius of Metz (9th century) or the *triplex modus corporis Christi* of Paschasius around the same time. In envisioning the three modes of Christ's bodily presence, we need not spiritualize away the call to Saul, "Saul, Saul, why are you persecuting me?" (Acts 9:4); nor are we ever excused upon hearing, "Whatever you did for one of these least brothers of mine, you did for me" (Mt 25:40).

Jesus, in His infinite promise, kept His word never to leave us orphans, to be with us until the end of time. The Word made flesh continues to live in the world, in that very Tabernacle, upon this very altar; but He chose to keep His promise of presence in such a way that demands our cooperation. Have you never stood before this sanctuary and asked, "Why are you so silent? Why are you so passive in the face of so much destruction in today's world, in this neighborhood, in these families which are crumbling, in my own heart?" Does it scare us to seek an answer? Do we instead hide behind the safety of structure and the pat-answers of piety?

In His wisdom, the Lord continues His visible and fleshy presence in this Eucharist, *but* this Host has no hands with which to feed the hungry, no feet with which to walk and visit the shut-in, no mouth to speak words of tenderness, no ears to listen to the lonely and startled. Jesus' presence here demands that we cooperate and complement the mode of His dwelling. These certainly are not easy words to encounter; they are rarely convenient to follow, but as Bishop Bossuet knew, "Jesus Christ bears us in himself; we are, if I may dare to say, more truly his body than his own body . . . whoever has the spirit of charity and of Christian unity will understand what I mean."[10] We shall understand this only when we deeply realize that we are called to be other Christs, to live our days as "unconscious Christs," as that divine eccentric, the English mystic Caryll Houselander puts it. We are no longer merely fallen creatures but in our Baptisms have been made Christ-bearers; and in light of our ordination, that vocation must be made real, public, fruitful.

Peter Julian Eymard asks, "How did you begin to love your mother? Sleeping within you, without sign of life, was a seed, an instinct, of love. Your mother's love awakened it; she cared for you, suffered for you, fed you with her body and by this generous gift you recognized her love."[11] The love planted in the Divine image of each of our souls is effected and elicited by the love of God. Our Mother Church gathers us each in to present us to the Father, reborn children within a new home and new purpose, all within a new family all because God Himself has assumed, personally and physically, our very human existence to Himself.

Mary's humanity, which God assumes to Himself in Christ, is fundamental; it is here divinity and humanity meet; and, thus, it is the same humanity the Christ gives us in Mary, His adopted brothers and sisters, her sons and daughters. This new life ushered in by the Son's Incarnation is, therefore, an interrelationship between Christ and the Church because the Son has come to identify His members with Himself, just as He did when He said, *"For I was hungry and you gave me food"* (Mt 25:35), and as He identified us with Himself when He called from heaven to the rampaging Saul who was persecuting God's holy people, *"Saul, Saul, why are you persecuting me?"* (Acts 9:4). "See yourself reflected in me," Christ says to each of us. Or as Gregory Nyssen writes, "Beholding the Church, one beholds Christ, as well."[12]

Pope Emeritus Benedict XVI united these two movements of our Eucharistic worship in *Sacramentum Caritatis* when he wrote that "the eucharistic mystery helps us to understand the profound meaning of the *communio sanctorum.* Communion always and inseparably has both a vertical and a horizontal sense: it is communion with God and communion with our brothers and sisters. Both dimensions mysteriously converge in the gift of the Eucharist."[13] But there is still a third movement, that movement into our own selves, our own experiences, our own hearts.

Inward as Mystery

The supreme manifestation of the Son's filiality takes place in darkness and in the cry from the Cross—here is the ultimate creed of His Church proclaimed: "Truly this man was the Son of God" (Mk 15:39). The Eucharist continues this ineffable trust between the Father and the Son while simultaneously ordering our loves and taming our fallen desire to rebel against God and His will for our lives: "Do you think that I cannot call upon my Father and he will not provide me at this moment with more than twelve legions of angels? But then how would the scriptures be fulfilled which say that it must come to pass in this way?" (Mt 26:53-54). The sacrifice of praise is a sacrifice of personal discovery, of coming in Christ to see not only who God is but who the human person is, as well. A young Joseph Ratzinger once admitted that when he was in distress and "would like to cry out as Job did," he was given the grace instead to "transform this cry into the word 'Father' and the cry . . . gradually [became] a word, a reminder to trust, because from the Father's perspective it is clear that [his] distress, yes, [his] agony, is part of the greater love for which [he gives] thanks."[14]

This movement from despair to trust is one that continued in Pope Emeritus Benedict's pontificate, as he translated the trust he related before the Cross to one before the Eucharist. This is a theme Pope Benedict used to invite young people to see in the Eucharist the story of their own lives, to discover the Eucharist as life's journey. It is in the "presence of the Sacred Host," he writes, that one begins one's "inner journey of adoration. In the Eucharist, adoration must become union."[15] Continuing, we learn that in the Eucharistic "hour" of Jesus' Passover, His hour becomes our hour, an opportunity to see who we are before the Father.

Here, we are invited to see our own worth, to see the many fragments of our lives collected into a purposeful whole, into a meaningful oblation! Here, the Father wants to console His children, to send the Spirit to penetrate our fear and our confusion, to let the Spirit overshadow His children and continue to incarnate His only Son. Here, before the Host, we can hear Christ say, in the words of Paul Claudel:

Come with me, where I am, in yourself,
and I will give you the key to life.
Where I am, there eternally is the secret of your origin...
Where are your hands that are not mine?
And your feet that are not nailed to the same cross?
I died and rose once and for all!
We are very close to one another...How can you separate yourself from me
without breaking my heart?[16]

No, for our hearts were meant to beat in unison. No longer is a personal relationship with Jesus enough; we were made not for a side-to-side alliance (*a relatio*) but for an internal living of His own life. For when we have finally died to the law, we slowly come to see that "yet I live, no longer I, but Christ lives in me" (Gal 2:20)! Or as Charles Williams so succinctly and perfectly expresses this *vis unitiva*: "Love you? I am you!"[17] Love unites, transforms, brings the other into the "I" creating an eternal "We."

The Mass is not a spectator sport; all the verbs of praise and sacrificial offering are in the first person plural. It is we who offer this *sacrificium laudis* and as *Lumen Gentium* put forward: "Taking part in the Eucharistic sacrifice, which is the fount and apex of the whole Christian life, [we] offer the Divine Victim to God, and offer [ourselves] along with It."[18]

All God's people offer this Host because this Host is the life of all the baptized. This is the unity we all desire—to know that we have been gathered and, thus, made beautiful and indispensable participants in the sacred offering. St. Thomas argues that since "unum, one, is a principle, just as good is a principle: hence everything naturally desires unity, just as it desires goodness and, therefore, just as love or desire for good is a cause of sorrow, so also is the love or craving for unity."[19] In this desire for unity from alterity, for communion through our own individuality, we catch a glimpse and a call of the Triune image in each of us. We all want to know we matter; we all want to see in another our eternal worth and in each other, sense our own fulfillment—to love and to be loved; this is the purpose of the human soul; this is the only purpose of the Incarnation.

St. Irenaeus knew that, "The Son undertakes all things as a ministry to the Father, from beginning to end."[20] As the filial offering of the Son to the Father, this Eucharist is a repudiation of all gnostic tendencies that see it necessary to divide God: a god who creates and a god who saves, a god who wrestles matter into some intelligible form and another god who liberates us from all body and relationality. For when the Spirit of God enters us, He finds not the virginal earth out of which He drew our first parents, but he rather finds a whole world of experiences and lifetimes, unique persons filled with eccentricities and foibles, burdens and regrets. Here, before the Blessed Sacrament, we must, thus, invite all to see themselves as they are—that the same Lord who created them is the same Lord who redeems them; the same God who gave each of us our own unique personalities, quirks, and desires is the same God who longs to consecrate and redeem every cell of our being, every pulse of our heart, everything we take for granted and even dislike about ourselves; here is both the unity we forfeited as well as the relationality we seek.

As mentioned earlier, the Graeco-Roman world in which the Messiah instituted the Eucharist was a world of individual strength and self-rule. An example is the two injunctions at Delphi: *Know Thyself* and *Nothing in Excess*. The lone individual reigned supreme and could achieve pagan perfection not only without others but precisely by eschewing the ecstasy and vulnerability personal relationship with others demands. For the Christian, on the other hand, self-knowledge is achieved precisely through personal interaction and communion with one outside him- or herself while virtue is not a self-help program wherein success or failure can be measured by the amount of food eaten or the number of truths told. No, the Christian life is defined by relationship, by otherness, by charity.

The Church is born solely from the person of Jesus Christ and, as such, the Church possesses absolutely no identity apart from Christ. The personality of the Church must be Christ's; the personality of the Church's ministers and all her baptized must be Christ's. On Holy Thursday, there appears a great reversal. Up to the Holy Triduum, the Church existed in Christ, hidden and latent. Yet, as Christ for the first time makes manifest His presence outside of Himself in the *appearances* of bread and wine, the Church is no longer in Him but He is now in the Church. The presence has not diminished and their closeness has not been weakened; but now, from the right hand of the Father, the Son both universalizes and deifies His presence in every soul.

Saint Augustine would have us look deeply at our own selves so as to understand the mystery of the Eucharist. By gazing at the sons and daughters, we come to know the Son; by examining the participatory mystical body, we catch a glimpse of the perfect Eucharistic body.

> So if you want to understand the body of Christ, listen to the Apostle telling the faithful, *You, though, are the body of Christ and its members*" (1 Cor 12:27). So if it is you that are the body of Christ and its members, it is the mystery meaning you that has been placed on the Lord's table; what you receive is the mystery that means you. It is to what you are that you reply Amen; and by so replying, you express your assent. What you hear, you see, is *The body of Christ*, and you answer, *Amen*. So be a member of the body of Christ, in order to make that Amen true.[21]

The Eucharistic sacrifice is of the whole Christ, body and head, Christ and Christians. It is on this very altar we must teach those whom we serve to see themselves, their lives, what they hold most dear. For here is every tear, smile, hope, and fear; here is every longing and all *eros* redeemed, unified into a life's story, made beautiful for all eternity. For if we continue to worship money, we are always going to feel poor; if we go on worshipping sex, we will always feel unloved; if we are allowed to think beauty or physical appearance will save us, we will keep on feeling ugly. Only the image of the Father in whose image we have been made can complete us; only He can quiet the restless heart and fill the God-sized hole in each of us. No career, no romance, no social standing will ever fully capture the human heart.

In a letter to his son, J.R.R. Tolkien held out the Eucharist as the one place where all the great loves converge, where all our desires meet. He wrote to his son Michael:

> Out of the darkness of my life, so much frustrated, I put before you the one great thing to love on earth: the Blessed Sacrament. . . . There you will find romance, glory, honour, fidelity, and the true way of all your loves on earth, and more than that: Death. By the divine paradox, that which ends life, and demands the surrender of all, and yet by the taste—or foretaste—of which alone can what you seek in your earthly relationships (love, faithfulness, joy) be maintained, or take on that complexion of reality, of eternal endurance, which every man's heart desires.[22]

A great paradox awaits: that on gazing upon the one who "had no majestic bearing to catch our eye, no beauty to draw us to him" (Is 53:2), we come to see how we are "the most handsome of men" (Ps 45:3), and the "most beautiful among women" (Sg 1:8).[23] Do not be surprised as you give yourself over to the Father as the Son if you begin to see the old ways no longer satisfying, your sins no longer beckoning; do not wonder why you have actually come to a love that longs to suffer for the other, for your people; do not be shocked as you begin to see yourself more and more another Christ, speaking words of love you have not rehearsed and swelling with a gratitude you did not even realize was yours.

Here is where the Eucharist moves from gratitude to hope, from realizing all God has done to all He is still to do. Whereas the theological virtues move us upward and outward, faith uniting us to the divine, charity propelling us toward our brothers and sisters, hope marks this third movement inward, enabling us to see that each of us is, in fact, that chosen beloved of the Father's, that each of us is that "just man" sung throughout the Scriptures. The virtue of hope is Eucharistic because both are the requisite sustenance for the *homo viator*, the pilgrim who still finds him or herself on the journey of life and who among the stumbles and pitfalls of any crossing, begins to wonder how things shall end.

All priests need to cultivate an awareness that a man can live such an extraordinary life only through extraordinary grace, not by being strong, but weak—ever reliant on the grace of Christ to live his life in and through Christ. Priests are called to be weak in Christ, not strong; be hopeful in Him, not assured in their own talents; be vulnerable before others, not always be the one who has to have the answer. Priests need to open their arms on the Cross of Life so all may know of the Father's covenanted care and undying love for all of His sons and daughters.

NOTES

1. Pope Benedict XVI, *Jesus of Nazareth: From the Baptism in the Jordan to the Transfiguration* (New York: Doubleday, 2007), 136-36.
2. Pope Paul VI, *Gaudium et Spes* (1965), sec. 24.
3. Thomas Weinandy, *Does God Suffer?* (Notre Dame: University of Notre Dame Press, 2000), 116.
4. *Jo. eu. tr.* 21.8; Rettig, vol. 2, 186.
5. C.S. Lewis, *Mere Christianity* (New York: MacMillan Co., 1958), 146-47.
6. *Catechism of the Catholic Church* (Washington, DC: USCCB Publishing, 2000), sec. 1359.
7. Ibid., sec. 1397.
8. *Catechism of the Catholic Church*, sec. 1397; John Chrysostom, Hom. in 1 Cor 27.4.
9. *Hom. in Mt* 50.3; PG 58.50 (my translation)
10. *Sermons sur la nécessité des souffrances* (for Palm Sunday), as in Henri De Lubac, *Catholicism* (Ignatius Press [1947] 1988) 99-100; this section is also where the triform body of Christ is outlined.
11. Peter Julian Eymard, *How to Get More Out of Holy Communion* (Manchester, NH: Sophia Press, 2000), 35-36.
12. Gregory of Nyssa, *In Cant.*, hom. 13; PG 44.1048 (my translation).
13. Pope Benedict XVI, *Sacramentum Caritatis* (2007), sec. 76.
14. Joseph Ratzinger, *Co-Workers of the Truth* (San Francisco: Ignatius Press, 1992), 311.
15. Pope Benedict XVI, Homily for the 20th World Youth Day in Cologne, August 21, 2005.
16. As quoted in John Paul II, *The Trinity's Embrace* (Boston: Pauline Books and Media, 2002), 398.
17. As in C.S, Lewis, *The Four Loves* (New York: Harcourt Brace 1988), 95.
18. Pope Paul VI, *Lumen Gentium* (1964), sec. 11.
19. *Summa Theologiae* I-II 36.3.
20. *Adversus Haereses* 4.6.3 (my translation).
21. *Sermo* 272; trans., Edmund Hill, Sermons, vol. 7 (Hyde Park, NY: New City Press, 1993), 300.
22. Letter to Michael Tolkein (6-8 March, 1941) as in *The Letters of J.R.R. Tolkien* (New York: Houghton Mifflin, 2000), 53-54.
23. See Benedict XVI, *Sacramentum Caritatis* (2007), sec. 35.

The Virtues of Sonship

Earl K. Fernandes

After making a retreat in Assisi, inspired by the example of Francis and Clare and at the suggestion of a priest friend, I read some sermons of another Franciscan—Anthony of Padua. In his Sermon for the Eighth Sunday after Pentecost[1], Anthony reflects on the Scripture: "Just so, every good tree bears good fruit, and a rotten tree bears bad fruit" (Mt 7:17). Anthony interprets this passage in a moral sense, applying it to life in the Spirit, noting that:

> a good tree consists of five things: roots, trunk, branches, leaves and fruit.... Naturalists tell us that the height of the tree corresponds to the depth of its roots.... A good tree symbolizes good will, which in order to last and be good, must also possess five things: first, the roots of humility, a trunk of obedience, branches of charity, leaves of holy preaching, and fruit of contemplation.[2]

Correspondingly, a short tree, one that does not reach up to the heavens, lacks these qualities. Using these metaphors, I will examine the virtue of sonship.

Roots of Humility

Anthony says that "the deeper the roots of humility are imbedded in the heart, the higher will rise the tree of good works. . . . Blessed indeed is that tree which has such roots, because it is from the roots that the tree bears fruit. The roots are symbols of humility because it springs up from good will in consequence of which a person will receive the fruit of eternal life."[3]

The word *humility* comes from *humus*, which means earth or ground. To be humble is to be conscious of one's lowly rank. "For you are dust, and to dust you shall return," (Gn 3:19) as Ash Wednesday reminds us. Commenting on Luke (1:14-15–"he will be great in [the] sight of the Lord"– Anthony explains: "*What a person is before God, that he is and no more.*"[4] This is a precise definition of humility.

Consider how Jesus humbled Himself, showing solidarity with sinners at His Baptism, being named by God for what He was and is—the Beloved Son. The virtues and identity of His Sonship are confirmed in the humiliation and suffering of His Passion, His dying naked, alone, and in weakness. In this humility, He saves. The humility of Christ is imbedded deep within His Sacred Heart. This is where our humility needs to be rooted—in the heart.

"*What a person is before God, that he is and no more.*"[5] In the Father's sight, we discover our identity—beloved sons. In truth and without pretense, we arrive at a true estimate of ourselves, admitting our utter dependence on Him; our relationship with Him (as sons to the Father) is the determining factor of our identity. Humility imparts knowledge of God and self, enabling us to see our true worth and to live as beloved sons, submissive to His will, to control our exaggerated sense of self-importance, rooted in fallen human nature. There is nothing weak about humility or about admitting that we need a Redeemer. It takes courage, that is, fortitude, to see ourselves as we are.

A chief barrier to humility is pride. Gregory the Great calls pride the mother of the capital sins, begetting the others.[6] The pride-filled person is of the opinion that his opinion is the only one that matters, whereas the Beloved Son of the Father is concerned with the Father's "opinion," His will. Self-sufficiency is a clear mark of pride. Humility is *what a person is before God, that he is and no more*.[7] Successes in life and in ministry also bring danger: the danger that "puffed up" by our successes, we may see ourselves as superior to our peers. This type of pride is a barrier to contemplation—to seeing God's face. Gregory writes:

> For they who seem themselves to be wise cannot
> contemplate the Wisdom of God . . . Because while
> the swelling of pride increases in their minds, it closes
> the eye of contemplation, and by considering that they
> outshine others, they then deprive themselves of the light
> of truth.[8]

We are not self-sufficient but in a relationship with the Father, the giver of every good gift who invites us to put those gifts at the service of others, as the Beloved Son washed the feet of His "beloved sons," the Twelve.

How does one cultivate humility? Gregory recalls Benedict's experience at Subiaco, when the devil tempted him to pride after the people there greatly esteemed him. Scorning worldly acclamations and pleasures, Benedict fled to his cave to pray, to be alone with God, and to receive instruction. This "monastic" humility demands detachment from worldly attractions and attachment to God. Immediately following Jesus' Baptism, when He is declared "the Beloved Son," He is driven into the desert by the Spirit—to acquire strength for mission. In the desert, self-denial, not so much renunciation of affections as renunciation of self-will, is necessary to cultivate humility.

The Trunk of Obedience

If humility forms the root of the tree, obedience—deriving from *obaudientia*—to pay attention or to listen—forms the trunk. Think of Samuel's words (1 Sm 3:1-10): "Speak, Lord, for your servant is listening" and, "Here I am. You called me." Obedience is the "strong" trunk that supports the branches, its leaves, and its fruits.

Obedience is a moral virtue by which we submit to legitimate authority and by which we are inclined to comply with the will of authority, even before a specific command is given or a reward is promised.[9] Consider Jesus' obedience at the home in Nazareth, despite His being the mighty God. As the beloved Son of Mary, He was obedient. As the Son of God, He was obedient—even in the darkness of Gethsemane. He was "obedient to death, even death on a cross" (Phil 2:8).

At the Last Supper, when Jesus spoke of obedience to His Apostles, He did so in the context of love: "This is my commandment: love one another as I love you. No one has greater love than this, to lay down one's life for one's friends. You are my friends if you do what I command you" (Jn 15: 12-14). Obedience is not a blind following. Obedience proceeds from love. Without love, obedience becomes slavish and demeaning. Jesus said, "As the Father loves me, so I also love you. Remain in my love. If you keep my commandments, you will remain in my love, just as I have kept my Father's commandments" (Jn 15: 9-10). Obedience begins with abiding, listening, and love.

In his Sermon for the Second Sunday of Advent, Anthony writes: "True obedience is humble in heart, respectful, prompt, joyful, and persevering."[10] Reflecting on the verse from Isaiah (Is 35:1-2)—"The wilderness and the parched land will exult; the Arabah will rejoice and bloom; Like the crocus it shall bloom abundantly, and rejoice with joyful song" (in some versions of the Bible, this passage reads "The wilderness shall bud forth and blossom, and shall rejoice full of praise")—he says: "the expression *bud forth* symbolizes the humility of heart of loving obedience, because a bud presages the coming flower. Humility is the beginning of every good work. Obedience should also be respectful, symbolized by the word *blossom*. From humility of heart respect comes forth, even in one's tone of voice."[11] What is your tone of voice when you speak to others—parishioners, brother priests, the bishop, employees? Is your tone of voice blossoming toward joyful praise? He continues: "Obedience ought also to be prompt and is symbolized by the word *rejoice*."[12] How quickly do you fulfill your duties out of love?

Obedience is demanded even in suffering. When Jesus was asked to endure His Passion, He said, "Let this cup pass from me; yet, not as I will, but as you will" (Mt 26:39). Though Jesus' Passion was rigorous, He was a willing Victim, suffering all things out of love. As such, He could joyfully say to the Good Thief, "Today you will be with me in Paradise" (Lk 23:43). Meditate on the joy Jesus experienced knowing that He had accomplished His mission as Son and Redeemer. The virtuous son submits to love and, so, experiences joy.

The Branches of Charity.

Rooted in humility and grafted on to the trunk of obedience, the tree stretches forth its branches—the branches of charity. When we no longer think about our own will, growth in charity begins. Love is about willing what is truly good for our neighbor. Sometimes, we fail to grow from boys to men—fail to grow from sonship to fatherhood—because we do not grow in charity. Our branches remain short. Two biblical stories illustrate the practice of charity and its connectedness to the virtue of joy as adopted sons of God: The Parable of the Rich Man (Mark 10:17-22) and The Parable of the Prodigal Son (Luke 15:11-32).

After reading these two stories, one might ask, "What keeps the branches of our charity from growing?" One barrier is worldly possessions. Obedience to the commandments is not enough for true joy. The rich young man has kept the commandments. He has done his duty, yet his heart longs for more. What more must he do? He must sell his possessions and follow Jesus. His face falls. Positively, his sadness offers hope for conversion—for eventual following. Negatively, his worldly comforts keep him from the radical charity that Gospel discipleship demands and from the experience of the deeper love Jesus offers.

As I was walking around Assisi during a retreat, I discovered in Francis that having less sometimes means becoming more—as a true son. Francis, in giving up wealth, in rejecting his earthly father's house, had God alone as his Father. The bishop who clothed Francis's nakedness represents the generosity of a father toward his beloved son. Francis became more and more human through his poverty, ultimately receiving even the wounds of Christ in his flesh. He had less, yet became more, possessing true riches in Christ Himself. This truth invites us to examine whether our worldly attachments keep us from experiencing the joy of being rich in Christ and of becoming beloved Sons of the Father. Does worldly wealth keep us not just from *doing* more but *being* more?

As sons, priests serve in the "Father's house." One chooses freely to serve or not. In the parable of the Prodigal Son, one son is foolish, squanders his wealth, lives a dissolute life, repenting and returning to his father's house. His vices are obvious, yet he remains son to his father. The other son of the father does his duty, yet his reaction to his father's generosity indicates he has not yet learned or received the virtues of mercy and charity from his father. His bitterness reveals his interior life. He has never really enjoyed being in his father's house or listening to his father's words. He has done his duty, but without love, without joy. As with Cain, jealousy rather than charity dominates his heart. He is not interested in being his brother's keeper or rejoicing with his father in his brother's return. The lack of love in his heart keeps his branches short. From his mistake, we learn to appreciate the blessings of the father to his beloved son: "All that I have is yours."

The Leaves of Holy Preaching

From the branches of charity grow the leaves—the leaves of holy preaching. Generally, priests are filled with charity, putting their lives at the service of God and the Church.

While charity is a virtue, so, too, is receptivity. Pope Benedict XVI writes:

> ...man cannot live by oblative, descending love alone. He cannot always give; he must also receive. Anyone who wishes to give love must also receive love as a gift. Certainly, the Lord tells us, one can become a source from which rivers of living water flow (cf. Jn 7:37-38). Yet to become such a source, one must constantly drink anew from the original source, which is from Jesus Christ, from whose pierced heart flows the love of God.[13]

Sons need to be humble enough to receive gifts from the Father, especially the gift of love. One of God's many gifts to us is His Word that comes to us in the Scriptures and in preaching. It is that same gift that priests hand on to others. How do sons of the Father use the gift of speech?

Take a moment, and listen to these lines of Scripture:

- "Everyone should be quick to hear, slow to speak, slow to wrath . . . " (James 1:19)

- "Set a guard, Lord, before my mouth, keep watch over the door of my lips." (Psalm 141:3)

- "No human being can tame the tongue. It is a restless evil, full of deadly poison." (James 3:8)

- "If anyone thinks he is religious and does not bridle his tongue but deceives his heart, his religion is in vain." (James 1:26)

Why has God given us our mouths? To sing His praises. To offer a word of compassion. To forgive. To be like Baranbas, a son of encouragement. To build up His Church with encouraging words as sins of the tongue are too common among priests.

There are sins like *cursing* and taking the Lord's name in vain, particularly in a moment of rage or frustration. Think about the sacredness of the name of God to the Jew. Think about the power of the name of Jesus. In His Name, we will cast out demons, lay hands on the sick and cure them, and be granted anything asked (Jn 14:14). There is power in the Holy Name.

The sin of *lying* consists of speaking a falsehood with the intention of deceiving. While telling little children to tell the truth, we often struggle to be a "cooperator in the truth." We tell small and big lies. Why? Do we not sometimes lie to make ourselves appear better than we are? We need to remember that humility is what a person is before God.

Yet another sin is *gossip*. Silence, rather than idle chatter, creates the environment for receptivity. The *Catechism of the Catholic Church* treats sins of the tongue under the eighth commandment because the *Catechism* speaks of three sins: rash judgment, detraction, and calumny. Why are these sins barriers to the virtues of sonship? The answer is: because they are contrary to the truth. The truth sets us free. Consider the serpent's dialogue with Eve in the Garden. It begins with a lie and ends with a lie. What does it bring? Sadness. Sorrow. Death. Jesus Himself is our joy; this same Jesus has revealed Himself as the Way, the Truth, and the Life. Honest, prudent speech—the leaves of holy preaching—is the virtue of the son.

The Fruit of Contemplation

"Every good tree brings forth good fruit." The fruit of contemplation brings joy to God's sons. Humble receptivity is critical for yielding the fruit of contemplation. If we are humble, obedient, filled with charity, and use our speech rightly, we will grow toward the heights of heaven—communion with God. While here below, we need, following the example of the Beloved Son, to be alone with the Father, coming to know the One in whom the heart discovers true joy. This means commitment to prayer. Alphonsus Liguori has two oft-quoted maxims: "*He who trusts himself is lost. He who trusts in God can do all things*" and "*He who prays will be saved. He who prays not will certainly be damned.*"[14]

Prayer is an absolute necessity to maintain communion with God, remembering that prayer is a conversation between the human heart and God. Alphonsus says that prayer is "nothing more than conversation between God and the soul in which the soul pours forth its affections, desires, fears, and petitions, and God speaks to the heart, causing it to know His goodness, and the love which He bears it, and what it must do to please him."[15]

Sometimes, we pray well. Other times, dryness abounds. Either way, it is important to give God what we can—our time and our hearts—and let Him do the rest. In this, we are offering Him the fruits, the first fruits, of our lives. When dryness persists, as sons of the Church, humbly recognizing our limits, we submit to the Church's liturgical prayer. Consolation comes knowing that the Church (in her members) is always at prayer. At times in the conversation, when we simply cannot find the words, perhaps God is trying to remind our souls of the need to listen *and* receive.

Receptivity is a hallmark of contemplation, as Alphonsus indicates: "While in meditation, a person goes out in search of God through the effort of reasoning. In contemplation, he gazes upon God Who has been found. In meditation, a person acts through the operations of his own faculties. In contemplation, God acts and the soul is acted upon, receiving the gifts infused into it by grace. The very light and the divine love which fill it make it lovingly intent upon contemplating God's goodness."[16]

Contemplation is that awareness of being in the presence of the One who loves you and whom you love. When there is an awareness of being in the presence of a loved one, there is a feeling of being one with that person. Love demands union with the beloved, and this love fills the heart with joy. God loves His sons.

"Every good tree bears good fruit, and a rotten tree bears bad fruit" (Mt 7:17). A good tree is a symbol of the righteous person who, in order to be good, must also possess five things: first, the roots of humility; second, a trunk of obedience; third, branches of charity; fourth, leaves of holy preaching; and fifth, fruit of contemplation.

NOTES

1.   Antonio di Padova, "Sermone di Domenica VIII dopo Pentecoste," in *I Sermoni*, 4th ed. (Padova: Messaggero di Sant'Antonio, 2005), 526-544.

2.   Ibid., 535: "*Osserva che nell'albero ci sono queste cinque parti: la radice, il tronco, i rami, le foglie e il frutto....I naturalisti infatti dicono che l'altezza degli alberi è pari alla profondità delle loro radici....L'albero buono simboleggia la buona volontà, alla quale, per durare ed essere buona, sono necessarie queste cinque cose: la radice dell'umiltà, il tronco dell'obbedienza, i rami della carità, le foglie della santa predicazione e i frutti, cioè la dolcezza della celeste contemplazione.*"

3.   Ibid., 535-536.

4.   Claude M. Jarmak, *If You Seek Miracles: Reflections of Saint Anthony of Padua* (Padova: Messaggero di Sant'Antonio, 1998), 119.

5.   Ibid.

6.   Gregory the Great, *Morals on the Book of Job*, transl. John Henry Parker (Oxford: J.G.F. and J. Irvington, 1844), vol. 3, book 31, sect. 87, 489-490.

7.   Jarmak, *If You Seek Miracles*, 119.

8.   Ibid., vol. 2, Book 14, sect. 64, 160.

9.   Jarmak, *If You Seek Miracles*, 130.

10.   Antonio di Padova, "Sermone di Domenica II di Avvento," in *I Sermoni*, 910: "*La vera obbedienza è umile, ossequiente, pronta, gioconda e perseverante.*"

11.   Ibid.: "*Umile nel cuore: questo indica la parola «germoglierà». Il germoglio è come l'inizio del fiore, e l'umiltà è l'inizio di ogni opera buona. Ossequiente nella voce, indicato dalla parola «crescerà». Dall'umiltà del cuore procede il rispetto, anche nel tono della voce.*"

12.   Ibid.: "*Pronta al commando, e a questo si riferisce la parola «esulterà».*"

13.   Pope Benedict XVI, *Deus Caritas Est* (2005), sec. 7.

14.   Alphonsus de Liguori, *Prayer, The Great Means of Obtaining Salvation* in *The Complete Works of Alphonsus de Liguori*, ed. Eugene Grimm, vol. 3, *The Great Means of Salvation and Perfection* (New York: Redemptorist Fathers, 1886-94; reprint ed., Brooklyn, 1927), 49.

15.   Alphonsus de Liguori, *The Way of Salvation and Perfection* in *The Complete Works of Alphonsus de Liguori*, ed. Eugene Grimm, vol. 2, (New York: Redemptorist Fathers, 1886-94; reprint ed., Brooklyn, 1927), 219. Here, Alphonsus is specifically referring to mental prayer or meditation.

16.   Alphonsus de Liguori, *Praxis confessarii* in *Theologia Moralis*, vol. 4, ed. Leonardo Gaudé (Rome: Typis Polyglottis Vaticanis, 1912), cap. IX, sec. 2, n. 126.

An Intimate Gaze: The Father with His Beloved Son, the Priest

Walter R. Oxley

"This is my beloved Son, with whom I am well pleased; listen to him" (Mt 17:5).

The voice of the Father in this great theophany of the Transfiguration declares the very words that the Father speaks daily to his priests and desires for his priests, in turn, both to accept and experience. As the ordained priest participates in the Sonship of Christ the Head, the Father daily calls him beloved, and affirms him in his daily ministry with the words, "With you, I am well pleased." Sadly, all too often, the priest is closed to experiencing this level of divine affirmation from the Father.

Image of Two Fathers: The Greater Father is the One Who Loves

Imagine two fathers of a family; both are able and adequate providers—stable and dependable and present. However, only one of the fathers gazes upon his children with love. At times, when he looks at them, when he captures them in a moment while they are eating or playing, or even gazing back upon him, his heart becomes engaged, and his whole being exclaims "My daughter!" or "My son!" The heart of the father then wells up with gratitude to the God the Father for the gift of this child with whom he has been entrusted. The second father certainly desires to give his child everything that the child needs, "What father among you would hand his son a snake when he asks for a fish? Or hand him a scorpion when he asks for an egg?" (Lk 11:11-12). The second father reflects this paternal solicitude and care in his vocation of fatherhood, but he is not capable of truly giving the gaze of love from the depths of his heart. Something is preventing him from being capable of both giving a gaze of love and from opening himself to experience the affective movements of non-spiritual and even spiritual consolation that accompany this experience. Is there not a deficiency in the second father? Is there not something present in the first father that is not present in the second? Would we not refer to the first father as truly a better dad because he sees his children from the perspective of love? "So faith, hope, love remain, these three; but the greatest of these is love" (1 Cor 13:13).

The Loving Gaze of the Earthly Father as Foundation for the Priest

The reception of the loving gaze from his earthly father certainly provides a foundation for the priest to welcome the receptive posture necessary to receive this loving gaze from his Father in heaven. However, sadly, many seminarians and priests have not been recipients of this loving gaze from their earthly father. With intentional and transparent spiritual direction directed at opening this wound for healing, the seminarian has the opportunity to receive the gaze from the Father for which he had either consciously or sub-consciously been longing.

Without experiencing the intimacy of the gaze of the
Father prior to his seminary formation, or within it, the
priest remains at great risk to live with a default image of
the Father whom he understands to be distant and angry.[1]
A trusted guide in the practice of spiritual direction, Fr.
William Barry, S.J. explains the default image of God in the
following manner:

> I find in my unguarded moments I have a "default"
> image of God. Almost without thinking I tend to beg
> for forgiveness for my past sins, or to beg for favors. I
> cringe interiorly when I imagine God knowing everything
> about me. So my almost spontaneous image of God does
> not feature what I have often seen in my loving parents,
> namely sheer delight in their children, enjoyment of their
> company. I do not easily transfer that image to God,
> at least as a "default" position. My "default," it seems,
> features God wagging a finger of blame at me, or at least
> looking at me with some unhappiness. I have noticed that
> many people have a similar "default" image of God. So
> while the words "God loves us" may trip off the tongue
> easily, they don't seem to have much of an effect on our
> "default" image of God.[2]

If this default image of the Father is never healed, and
the priest's true relationship with Father as his son rightfully
discovered, restored, and healed, the priest remains suscep-
tible to being bound by an unnecessary duty-determined
vision of the priesthood. This vision of the priesthood is
often marked by an excessive scrupulosity and perfectionism,
and an exaggerated tendency to receive approval and affirmation from either his peer group, or from other pseudo-father

figures in his life whom he has elevated in order to receive the fatherly affirmation which he so deeply desires.

Receiving the Gaze in the Form of a Personal Name

The invitation for all Christians but, perhaps, most especially for priests, is both to accept and experience the paternal gaze of outpoured and overflowing love that is occurring incessantly between the Father and the Son in the Holy Spirit in the relationally constituted immanent life of the Holy Trinity. As the priestly ordination conforms the priest to Christ the Head, there is certainly a moral imperative for the priest to live a life that reflects this identity; but is it not even more primary and, perhaps, even more necessary to identify an objectively new form of relationship with the Father by which the priest is a recipient of the newly given gaze of love, even prior to his administering a single priestly act?

Fr. Herbert Alfonso, S.J., in his book *Discovering Your Personal Vocation: The Search for Meaning through the Spiritual Exercises,* speaks of the Father electing us and giving us a particular name. Fr. Alfonso states:

> In 1965 I had such an overpowering experience of the Spirit during my annual eight-day retreat, which worked a complete overhauling and transformation in my personal life and ministry, that I have continued to live out this single greatest grace of my life, and to draw out unceasingly the rich strands of that grace for the true understanding, practice and direction of the Spiritual Exercises of St. Ignatius. A seminal gift and grace, I like to call it in fact, as I am drawing on it for ever fresh new vistas that open out for me in the field of theology and spirituality, and in my ministry of the

Spirit. The central nucleus of a rich personal synthesis for life and ministry is what it has come to be. What I have characterized above as the single greatest grace of my life is that 1965 retreat I discerned my truest and deepest "self," the unrepeatable uniqueness God has given me in "calling me by name." And I have come to realize that the discernment of that truest and deepest "self" is the authentic, the most profound and radical meaning of the "election" which is the goal of the Ignatian Exercises. This truest and deepest "self," this God-given uniqueness, I call the "personal vocation." Besides, my own personal experience and my ministry of the Spirit have taught me that the deepest transformation in any person's life takes place in the actual living out of this very "personal vocation."[3]

If the intimacy and familiarity of being called by a name is a manner of expressing closeness and establishing interpersonal connection with the other by way of language,[4] how much more so does the Father want to call His son, the priest, by a personal name? Firstly, has the seminarian or priest accepted the desire of the Father for him to experience his beloved sonship by revealing to him in prayer the particular name revealing how he is gazed upon? Secondly, is the priest open to the possibility of being called by a particular name that suits him personally, as well as to the possibility of this reality being accepted and experienced in prayer? Only when this occurs is the priest truly able to be free from the burden of thinking that he is never meeting the Father's expectations of him.

The Priest as Loved in His Imperfection

How sad when a priest is burdened with the thoughts of
a Father never being pleased with him. As he remains shack-
led with incessant thoughts of imperfection, of not being
good and holy enough, he never is able to place himself in
the necessary posture of vulnerability and receptivity needed
both to accept and experience the reality that he is loved in
his imperfections and inadequacies, in his falling short of
reflecting the life of Jesus, a place where he should not be
ashamed but, on the contrary, truly a place of deep understanding for the Father, and a place where the Father wants
to live and dwell with the Holy Spirit. Essentially, when one
is beloved, imperfections, weaknesses, inadequacies—even
his struggle against sin—make him more of an object of
love. For the gaze of a loving earthly father is given to a
child equally to areas of deficiency and need as it is to areas
of strength. Therefore, the priest who lives the moral life,
prays regularly, and is intentionally and actively engaged in the
struggle against sin truly has nothing to fear.

Without the experience of this depth of affirmation from
the Father in prayer, we have the very probable reality of a
priest who diligently fulfills all of the duties and responsibilities required of him by his priestly office but who, at the
same time, is consistently living with the pained experience of
being guilty, somehow always living with the feeling that he is
not living up to what the Father truly demands of him. While
experiencing some psychological consolation from his priestly
ministry, he lives in a consistent state of spiritual desolation,
always feeling as if he is not worthy of experiencing the love

that the Father desires for him to experience throughout his day.

The Danger of Not Experiencing the Love of the Father for the Diocesan Priest

Only with a lived awareness of the gaze of the Father is an authentic priestly spirituality able to emerge and develop. Otherwise, affirmation will be sought by the priest within his own peer group. Without experiencing affirmation by the Father, he will seek to receive it elsewhere, and this behavior will become most acutely noticed. If a priest has not accepted and experienced the love of the Father, he may seek to impress his peer group, touting his successes in parish development and reform. In such cases, however, is he not misdirected in seeking affirmation from that source? Is he truly capable of loving the Church not for his own popularity and higher profile status within the Church, but as a hidden, humble, and largely unnoticed father of a large and poor family? When the diocesan priest seeks affirmation from the wrong place, the parish staff, and the lay faithful themselves, can easily become regarded not as pilgrims on their own spiritual journey from, in, and returning to the Father, but as obstacles, or even as trophies marking the victory of a conquest. In these unfortunate situations, the New Evangelization often comes at the cost of excessive inter-personal collateral damage that may exceed any potential long-term fruits for the renewal of the parish.

The Diocesan Priest: Called To Live in an
"Intimate and Unceasing Union with the Holy Trinity"

Tragically, there exist too many priests who are devoutly attentive to their duties and responsibilities and would certainly respond, in most cases, very favorably to their level of psychological happiness within the priestly ministry who, nevertheless, continue to live in a place of spiritual desolation. Priests who, while being very devout, if asked if they have either experienced or even believe in the possibility of living as *Patores Dabo Vobis* states, in "intimate and unceasing union with the Holy Trinity,"[5] would far too often answer, "No," on both counts. Essentially, both the reality and the potentiality would be foreign to far too many priests. In contrast to the number of hours that the priest spends sanctifying and bringing salvation to others through the sacraments is the stark possibility that, while giving his life, he, at the same time, may never experience the reality of his being gazed upon intimately as a beloved son of the Father, His priest. The deepest desires of the Father for each priest, however, are eternally unchanging. "'This is my beloved Son, with whom I am well pleased'" (Mt 3:17).

NOTES

1. William A. Barry, S.J. "Changing the 'Default' Image of God," *Human Development* 26, no. 1 (2005): 28.

2. Ibid.

3. Herbert Alphonso, S.J, *Discovering Your Personal Vocation: The Search for Meaning Through the Spiritual Exercises* (New York: Paulist Press, 2001), 2.

4. See the Jewish philosophers F. Rozenzweig, *The Star of Redemption*, pgs. 175-176, 1971; and M. Buber, *I and Thou*, pg. 112, 1923 for more on the power of the use of the name in divine and human language (Rozenzweig) and on the relational imperative in philosophy.

5. See John Paul II, *Pastores Dabo Vobis* (1992), sec. 45. The priest is called to both an "intimate" and "unceasing union with the Trinity." See *Pastores Dabo Vobis*, secs. 12 and 16 for the source of the priest's identity is in the Blessed Trinity. See *Pastores Dabo Vobis*, sec. 33 for priestly holiness as understood as "intimacy with God."

CPSIA information can be obtained
at www.ICGtesting.com
Printed in the USA
FSOW01n2042050216
16631FS